The Magpie Art

Gathering the Brightness
of Every Day

T0309034

GREEN WRITERS PRESS   *Brattleboro, Vermont*

The Magpie Art

GATHERING THE BRIGHTNESS OF EVERY DAY

Paul Weinfield

Printed in the United States

10 9 8 7 6 5 4 3 2 1

Green Writers Press is a Vermont-based publisher whose mission is to spread
a message of hope and renewal through the words and images we publish.
Throughout we will adhere to our commitment to preserving and protecting
the natural resources of the earth. To that end, a percentage of our proceeds
will be donated to environmental activist groups and The Southern Poverty Law
Foundation. Green Writers Press gratefully acknowledges support from individual
donors, friends, and readers to help support the environment and our publishing
initiative. Green Place Books curates books that tell literary and compelling
stories with a focus on writing about place—these books are more personal
stories/memoir, spiritual books, and biographies.

GREEN PLACE BOOKS   GReen writers press

Giving Voice to Writers & Artists Who Will Make the World a Better Place
Green Writers Press | Brattleboro, Vermont
www.greenwriterspress.com

ISBN: 978-1-7320815-1-2

COVER DESIGN & ILLUSTRATION:
PETER MENDLESUND

Dedicated to my teacher, Peter Doobinin,
with love and gratitude

CONTENTS

PREFACE

THIS IS A BOOK OF ENCOURAGEMENTS. In our advertising culture, we have largely come to regard encouragements as insincere or, at best, ineffective. We walk around all day not really believing the inspiration we trade in, our heads full of discouraging thoughts, and all the while, we tend to forget: *We are always listening to ourselves.* This is a book that explores how our lives are changed by the words we say and think.

This is not a primer on meditation or Buddhism, but the reader will quickly see how highly I value the practice of mindfulness of breath as a way of getting encouragements to "stick." Just as a tattoo artist might use a needle to get ink under someone's skin, so too, I have found, mindfulness of breath is the best way to help encouraging words go "straight to the heart," as the Thai ajaans say. The reader might find it helpful to practice a bit of breath meditation before or after reading each of the following passages. Read slowly, and try to practice whatever you find of value.

Finally, this is a book about teaching yourself "from the middle"— from the middle of frustration or joy or boredom or wherever else you find yourself today. It is a book with a single thesis: that there is always something you can do, moment by moment, to discover the brightness of your life.

I hope it brings some benefit and peace.

PAUL WEINFIELD
New York City, 2018

1. ∾ The Magpie Art

Live your life as a magpie builds her nest, gathering the bright moments of each day. If you can connect one light to another, you can build a home for yourself in this world.

LOVE

(spring)

2. ∾ Wading into an Ocean

Be patient with your heart, for you will not find unconditional love all at once. You will not discover it in a person you meet or in the sudden beauty of the springtime leaves. Every experience, profound though it may be, has its terms and conditions, and what we are seeking is not experience at all, but something we can only deepen into gradually, imperceptibly at times, year after year, like a bather slowly wading into an ocean. We deepen every time we see the illusion of the conditions we place on love. Once again, the beloved's hand withdraws, the leaves shrivel, and yet something remains unchanged. Once again, we notice this, and with each new noticing, we take one more small step into the sea.

3. ∾ Love Does Not Fit into This World

Love does not fit into this world. We spend so much time managing relationships and improving ourselves in the hopes of making love "work" that we forget that what we are searching for is something larger than anything a single life could contain. Even if you spend the rest of your days in the arms of your beloved, there will always be moments when, watching this person asleep, perhaps, you realize you are in the presence of something you will never get to the bottom of, something you can feel but never fully touch, something you desperately want both to grasp and let go, like children who catch fireflies just to throw them back into the sky where they shine.

And in these moments when you realize that love does not fit, you must learn not to panic or to blame anyone for the awkwardness you feel. You must find a way, rather, to be grateful for the limitlessness of love, for the distance at which it stands, precisely so that it can guide us, for the way that love is forever, even though we are not.

4. ❧ Messengers of Your Own Goodness

Watch how you subtly reject love when it comes to you in unfamiliar forms: the smile of a stranger on the street, the good wishes of a relative you never were that close to, the affection of someone you hoped would be your lover but turned out to be your friend. There are a million things we ought to say no to in this life, but love, in any form, is never one of them. Saying yes to love does not mean getting into tangled relationships or giving away time you don't have or forcing yourself into false intimacies. It simply means treating everyone who comes to you bearing affection as a messenger of your own goodness and the goodness of life itself, as though each of these beings were carrying a single syllable that forms a part of the great love letter that you will read some day and understand was meant for you.

5. ❧ Precious, Not Special

What if love isn't special? What if it's as ordinary and all-surrounding as the sky or the sea? Then to cherish it would mean not to promote it or lift it from the crowd, but to enjoy it as one enjoys a simple thing: to delight in an eternal expectedness that has no day or name or color; to treat it as a familiar stranger who leaves no memory because he never leaves; to be sure love will mean the same thing when we meet in some future time, when you'll await me at your table and I'll await you at mine.

6. ∽ Dreaming in a Foreign Language

In the end, feeling loved is something you have to learn for yourself, like a foreign language. Most people come to love searching for someone who already speaks their language. But your capacity to grow and deepen into love requires that you learn new ways of expressing it: new gestures, new symbols, new forms of communication. When you learn a foreign language, at some point you have to let go of its rules and assume you are able to understand. I remember falling asleep once in Morocco and imagining, in my dream, that I understood what the gardeners outside were saying in Arabic. And when I woke, I found I actually did understand. Love is like that. So today, as you observe people in streets, stores, and restaurants, imagine that all of them are trying to communicate the deep love that they feel — because they are, whether they know it or not. And then look to your heart to see if you don't feel that much more loved, that much more touched by the kindness that, visible or not, is everywhere.

7. ∽ There Is No Substitute for Paying Attention

There is no substitute for paying attention. As we move through life, we develop all sorts of shortcuts for finding happiness: daily routines, preferences, bits of wisdom we accumulate like Post-it notes. The problem isn't that these things are false, for they often contain a fair amount of truth, but that we relate to them with ignorance about the mind's role in creating happiness. We forget that the value of what we do also depends on the attitude we bring to doing it: the nourishment of food depends on the nourishing intentions we bring to eating; human companionship heals according to the healing intentions we bring to meeting. And so the most important habit you must develop is the habit of asking yourself, "What would be an act of self-love right now?" As my teacher says, the true answer to that question is often the opposite of the loud words in your head: if a voice says you should indulge in sense-pleasure, restraint might be the most loving action; if a voice says work harder, resting might be the most loving action. Try to think a bit less and focus on your breath a bit more. If you can feel how the life in your lungs wants to move, you will learn a lot about how to take care of yourself.

8. ∾ PRACTICING INTIMACY

Intimacy is not something you find, but something you practice. We all want safe spaces in which we can be vulnerable, but if you don't develop a safe place in your mind, no amount of external reassurance will make you feel protected enough to let down your guard. Meditation, yoga, therapy—these all can be helpful in developing a sense of inner refuge. But at some point, you have to take risk in your personal life. You have to practice every day, in some small way, showing those you love what is most difficult in you. And to do that, you first have to be clear that you didn't ask to have your feelings. You didn't choose your difficult emotions, just as you didn't choose your parents, and while you might at times be embarrassed by both, you have a right and an ability to live a life that is separate from both. People talk a lot about "taking responsibility for emotions," but the irony is that you can't take responsibility for what you feel until you begin to identify with it less. So today, try to share some part of yourself with someone who is reasonably safe—but just as important, find a safe attitude of mind from which to do that sharing. We all want to be loved for who we truly are, but you don't just wake up one day to find that has happened. To be loved for who you are, you have to practice being who you are.

9. ∾ LOVING FROM A DISTANCE

Learn how to love from a distance. True intimacy, unlike the constant contact our culture teaches, requires that we withdraw into ourselves long and deeply enough to remember what love feels like in our bodies and inner lives. Despite our best-laid plans, too much contact causes love to change from a reality into an idea about how the other person should be or behave. But love is not an idea: it is a real thing you can feel wherever you are, far or near, only you must practice learning to feel it. So today, take some time alone to call to mind someone you love, and picture that person apart from you, smiling, resting, at ease. And then try to feel in your chest, as you would any physical sensation, the wish that you have for this person to be happy, whether or not you are there to share in that happiness. If a sense of loss or panic arises, remind yourself that you are traveling to a place where you and those you love can be together completely, beyond the limitations of words or ideas or even time itself: a meeting place in the heart that only separation can reveal.

10. ∾ LOVE FOR WHAT HAS NOT YET BORNE FRUIT

Perhaps the greatest love is love for what has not yet borne fruit. It is easy to rejoice in success or distance yourself from failure, but much harder to see that there are parts of your life already in tune with your deepest desires, but whose time has not yet come. Ask yourself what you are doing right now that feels right (though its impact is still invisible) and watch over these latent parts of yourself, not by forcing them to be strong, but by simply being with them, as you would a sick child who needs your attentiveness more than any medicine. Your hypotheses about what makes you happy may prove wrong some day, but no matter: the love you will have learned from seeing things through will be worth all your errors.

11. ✦ LOVING BEYOND YOUR MEANS

We know we have to love ourselves. The trouble is, we think self-love is a prelude to something else, like an appetizer that comes before the main course of loving others. People often think: *I should love myself so I will be more attractive to the ones who will make me happy.* In this way, they throw their self-love away. If we look at most of our relationships, we see that, in them, we are often loving beyond our means—that is, we are trying to give to others what we ourselves do not have, and feeling anxious as a result. So today, spend the better part of your energy cultivating love for yourself. You don't have to take anything away from anyone else. Just develop the perception that you are worthy of your own affection whether or not it brings you gain, status, praise, or pleasure from others. What would that actually feel like? When you find the answer to that question in your heart, you will have found a gate that opens in all directions.

12. ✦ BUILDING AND SELLING A HOUSE

In their loneliness, people often say, "But I have so much love to give!" And it's true: they do. But the way out from loneliness doesn't just depend on giving love; it also depends on healing the cracks in the mind through which love keeps escaping. To do this, rest from your habit of trying to make others feel your love. For building a house and selling it are two different matters, though we often perceive them as one.

13. ✦ THE SPIRIT OF ADVERTISING

You don't have to push your light out into the world. We live in an age clouded by the spirit of advertising, an age in which we not only believe the message of certain ads, but also believe, on some level, that convincing others to want what we have is the highest goal of human existence. Whether as artists seeking to brand our-selves or people participating in a dating culture that values mar-keting over intimacy, we fall for the trap of thinking we need to trick others into needing us. And when we are filled with the spirit of advertising, we fail to see the deep loneliness that comes from getting up each morning and trying to sell what was always free to begin with. This is why we practice generosity, not just to help others, but to help ourselves remember that we have an inner goodness, an inner light that will always travel out into the world, without money or marketing or coercion, if we only let it shine. So today, when you find yourself trying to convince someone else of your worth, make generosity your ally. Be generous with your time, your energy, and your vulnerability. Be great, but give your greatness away freely. If you can do that, you will find yourself prized above all the jewels in the world.

14. ∾ Generosity Is a Muscle

Generosity is a muscle. If you use it only in sudden bursts, after long periods of inactivity, you are going to feel sore. We are always asking, "How can I be generous when others are trying to take advantage of me?" While of course there are times when it isn't wise to give, what makes an act of generosity healthy or unhealthy has more to do with how you've trained yourself to view it than with how others behave. The more out of shape you are when it comes to giving, the more you will experience giving as an unpleasant exertion and feel resentful when situations aren't perfectly reciprocal. As with physical training, the best way to develop strength in generosity is to prize consistency over quantity of effort. You don't need to empty out your bank account or spend your one day off slaving for someone else. You can be generous not only with your money, but with your attention, your appreciation, your knowledge, your forgiveness, your fearlessness. You can be generous wherever your heart feels inspired. So today, try to give more, in smaller amounts. You will make mistakes sometimes and feel hurt. But you will heal too. Your heart, like your body, is meant to be used.

15.∾ THE MIRAGE OF EXPERIENCE

We are born with a longing to dive deeper into life, yet we keep on colliding against the mirage of experience. Something in us wants depth to take the form of a new lover or new country, even though we know on some level that all experiences have happened already and will keep happening without any dimension to them. The yielding water we are searching for doesn't lie in what is unknown but, always, in what is already known. Lean more closely into your old joys and sorrows. There is your river. There is your depth.

16. ∾ REAL POLITICS

Forget about changing the world. You can only change the one life you've been given. If you're lucky, the love and compassion you cultivate in the brief time you're here will find a way to inspire, educate, organize, and heal many people, but there are no guarantees. One thing is sure: you will accomplish a lot more good if you can see your actions in terms of generosity rather than in terms of trying to make a mark on the world. For just as there is joy in offering food to someone, whether or not he accepts, there is joy in all work if you can see it as a gift rather than something the world has to accept. Don't let your sense of purpose be influenced by television, which shows us faraway things about which we can do very little. There is plenty to do right here. Listen to someone's problems. Try to get to the bottom of your anger. Learn how to apologize. These are political acts too.

17. ∾ Make a Present of Your Mind

Strive to develop the non-physical forms of generosity. You have more to give this world than the money in your pocket or your habits of consumption. You have within you the gift of your attention, the gift of your care, the gift of your fearlessness, the gift of your forgiveness—so hone these gifts and start to know their worth. In Thailand, there is a day on which monks, who have no possessions, go before the king to make him a "present of their minds." We forget sometimes that even those with political or physical power still must rely upon the goodwill of others. Society can go from order to chaos in the blink of an eye, and all that keeps the social order intact is our innate, though often buried, sense of generosity. So today, start to see the power you have in the intentions you bring to every moment. Ask yourself, "What can I give right now?" And then look, look as your heart shows you possibilities your mind has not yet grasped.

18. ∾ The Shells of Some Oysters

Life doesn't always let us find goodness in the people and things we hoped to find it in, but it does give us opportunities to find that goodness somewhere. The shells of some oysters never open, but those are the ones that probably would have made us sick anyway.

19. ∾ Those Who Still Are There in the Morning

If you want to find stability in your life, test the components of your life to see if they are truly stable. Try stepping away from your relationships, your work, your opinions, and your dreams to see which ones crumble as soon as you let go. While there may be worthwhile parts of your life that are not yet ready to be released, like children who still need training wheels or puppies that still need leashes, the point of life is not to go from leash to leash or from one set of training wheels to another, but to begin to know the deeper permanence that all objects of love, impermanent though they may be, nevertheless point to. So today, pick a few things you decide you are not going to work on: try going a day without one of your practices, without engaging with someone you routinely engage with, without thinking about something you routinely think about. It is only by testing things that we discover we are free. And it is only by giving ourselves to the uncertain night that we discover who is still there in the morning.

20. ∾ As a Baker Tests Bread

We are not merely forgetful beings. We lose our way, but we have the ability to keep the most important things in mind across weeks and years. You have been working at this life for a long time now. Start to develop faith in your ability to navigate by how you feel. Put away some of your calendars and books, and watch over the direction of your days the way a baker watches over bread, neither testing it too often nor forgetting it entirely. For the things we have to do to care for ourselves are fewer than we might think, but we have to do them over and over again, in a steady rhythm of unbroken simplicity.

21. ∾ The Power of Your Simplicity

Have faith in the power of your simplicity. We sometimes think playing hard to get is the basis of power. Maybe in one sense it is: playing hard to get gives us the power to attract people who see in our aura of mystery an opportunity to enact their worst patterns. As for the ones we really want, playing hard to get just makes them shrug their shoulders and walk away, wondering why something as simple as love had to be so complicated. We play hard to get with ourselves too, for in those moments when we recognize true happiness in our lives—a happiness that doesn't depend on being or possessing anything—the mind tends to hold back a part of itself, thinking, "This is too ordinary; I shouldn't commit all my efforts right here." So we need to remind ourselves that what is extraordinary is always found by investigating what is ordinary: this body, this breath, this moment and all its untapped potentials for goodness. Try to live this day as do flowers of the field, which do not worry about whether they are special, or withhold their colors to increase their value. The flowers simply bloom, and in blooming, are miraculous.

22. ∾ LET LOVE DO ITS WORK

Effort made from the heart is never wasted. If you have a job that pays only once a month, you know that every hour you work comes back to you eventually. You don't get discouraged if no one hands you a wad of cash after each task you perform. Yet when it comes to effort made from the heart, we expect immediate results. Someone says, "Try to meet your experience with love, each and every moment," and you say, "I did that, and I still feel horrible." But loving intentions are like an ointment, to use Ajaan Lee's analogy: if you put them on a wound and then wash them off right away with your impatience and self-doubt, the ointment never has a chance to seep into your body and do its work. So today, try to think thoughts of goodwill for yourself and others, and follow these up with the thought, "Now let me let love do its work." And as you reflect on the perfect conservation of energy that exists in the heart, you will start to feel something happening, moment by moment, intention by intention, in your body. We find what we are looking for, so make sure to look for what you most want to find.

23. ∾ TREES BEFORE THE RAIN

How you relate to making effort is how you relate to love. If you withdraw from the work you have to do, love will seem to withdraw from you. If you try to push ahead, love will seem to push ahead of you. For love is not just the product of our efforts, but a quality that must be present in those efforts themselves if they are to lead anywhere good. And so it is that all tasks, great and small, are part of the training of the heart. So today, whatever you do, develop effort in tune with love. Have you seen trees before the rain, how they seem to turn up their leaves to receive water from the sky? The trees do not grasp at what is to come, nor do they try to keep it from coming; they simply change with the changing moment, and in doing so, are free. And inside you, too, there is one who is already changing to meet the future you've been waiting for. Let that one guide you through your work today. That one knows where love is to be found.

24. ∾ The Hole at the Bottom of Your Cup

As we get older, we see the many ways that inner and outer goodness diverge. You might want to help your partner financially, but don't have enough money; you might want to comfort a friend, but can't take away his pain; you might want to express yourself creatively, but lack the audience or support. Adulthood shows us the limits of doing good on a purely external level and the danger that comes from thinking we are lovable only because of what we do with our physical bodies. At some point you have to turn from the unreliable praise and success on which you have built your self-worth and start to acknowledge your inner goodness — the goodness you were born with (though you still must cultivate it) before you ever earned the praise of others. You were born with generosity, and you can give to the present moment with nothing other than your heart and your kind attention. You were born with goodwill, and you can wish others well even when you cannot help them. You were born with creativity, and you can live an inspired life just by listening to the voice that is great within you. So don't waste your life trying to fill your cup with good things without ever seeing the hole you keep tearing into the bottom.

25. ❧ FORCING AND FINDING

Rid yourself of the idea that hard work is the reason you deserve to be happy. Our minds are forever tricking us into believing that happiness is something we have to earn or produce from scratch. But just as you didn't build the computer you work on or the body you are living through, yet you know how to use these things even without full knowledge of their mechanics, so too you don't have to make the love and joy and contentment that are hard-wired into your existence out of nothing. Your "work" (if you must call it that) is not to force these things into being, but to find them, and to trust that they are there even when you misplace them, like a set of keys that must be in your house somewhere if that's where you last left them. Your house is your fathom-long body: search there. Bring your awareness to your body and notice which parts feel good. And then reflect that what feels good is something basic to who you are. Let your focus on the small pockets of ease you find in your hands or feet or throat lead you into the fuller bliss that is your birthright, just as small rivers join up with the sea. Gratitude is the key — not just gratitude for your house or job, but for the million points of light within you that are forever leading you home.

26. ❧ NO NEWS TO SHARE

You must believe in your life even when you have no news to share: no job offers, no revelations, no letters of acceptance. We all want to be loved for who we are, and our desire to share news is often an expression of our wish for others to see us in a certain light. But we put ourselves in a vulnerable position this way, for others are free to fail to see us as we are, free to misunderstand us, free to be indifferent. And so you must remember that you are greater than the sum of all your experiences. You are working on a life whose progress cannot be seen only in what you have gained or accomplished, just as a camera cannot fully capture the growth of a plant or child. One day there are seeds, then suddenly sprouts. So today, do your best to sow seeds of love in your heart. Your love for yourself and others may not seem newsworthy, but it is the source of all the good news that ever has been, or ever will be.

27. ∞ MORE CHOICES

Try to make more choices in the course of your day. In our culture, we tend to confuse real choice, which takes place in the mind, with consumer preferences. We think we have fixed desires that can only be satisfied by the right products, the right people, or the right experiences. And so we find ourselves in a perpetual state of waiting on this delivery or that lover or the world to change. But if you want to be free, you have to see that your choices create your desires, not just the other way around, and you have to make an effort to choose more often and more skillfully: to choose to focus on beauty as you walk down the street, to choose to see the best in others and in yourself, to choose, above all, to see that you always have choices. Think of your day as a screenwriter would, in terms of scenes that each involve a choice your character must make. As you enter a store or an office or the vicinity of someone who is difficult for you, ask yourself, "What are my choices?" Usually, the important choices will take place inside you, on the level of your attitude: "Can I choose to meet this experience with love?" "Can I choose to see the work I have to do today as an expression of care for myself?" Your choices are both infinite and infinitely powerful, but you will not find the important ones on a menu or in a sales catalog. Use your ingenuity. Use your heart.

28. ❧ Room to Hear the Call

If you want to find your calling in life, you have to make room in your life to hear the call. We often have overly mystical ideas about what makes a life of purpose, as though it were a matter of entering a church or attending a seminar or disappearing to Bali for good. But in reality, your ability to hear the voice that is great within you depends mainly on how you carry yourself in everyday conversations, for your outer speech is only ever a mirror of your mind. If you interrupt others, you will interrupt your inner guidance. If you speak harshly, you will be afraid to listen to yourself. If you speak falsely, you'll never believe anything you think. So today, take a deeper look at how you use words. No matter how tedious or insignificant your conversations may seem, remind yourself that, through them, you are making space for a higher wisdom. Don't treat these moments as your day job, when what you've always wanted was a vocation.

29. ❧ Your Life's Work

Whatever you think is keeping you from doing your life's work is your life's work. Every distraction, anxiety, or doubt that keeps you from learning some deeper lesson is itself the deeper lesson. The mind that we bring to the surface of life is the same one we bring to its core, and so there is no errand or chore unrelated to the person you are trying to become. As you move through this day, try not to struggle against the incompleteness of your time and effort, but offer your whole heart to whatever is at hand. It is in giving this way that we see how much we have to give.

30. ❧ The Mouth of the Trail

You are standing at the right spot. All your insecurities, petty jealousies, and annoyances—these are not distractions from the great journey you have been wanting to make. These *are* the journey, which proceeds not along some high mountain pass, but in the shape of a spiral, circling around and deepening into the present moment. Your path is simpler than you think: all you have to do, when difficult emotions arise, is turn to these feelings and regard them as your fate, to recognize that they could never have been otherwise, and to hold yourself in compassionate understanding. So today, when you are struggling, remind yourself: "This is the mouth of the trail. This is the only way anyone ever makes it to the goal." Let your feet sink into the earth, right where you are. For the end of all exploring, as T.S. Eliot said, "will be to arrive where we started and know the place for the first time."

31. ∾ THE MASTERPIECE IN THE MARBLE

There is a place in your heart where what you desire most and what you already have are one and the same. The art of desire is to chip away at what we think we want in order to reveal our longing for what already is, just as the art of sculpture, Michelangelo said, is to chip away at a block of marble until the masterpiece within it comes forth. We chip away at our ordinary desires by learning to feel them in our bodies, as one might feel any physical sensation, for it is within our bodies that desire can attach to love rather than anxiety. Your wish for money, for example, will always cause you stress, for it is based on an undependable object, yet your underlying desire for security aims at what you already can feel within you. So today, use the phrase "so I can feel" to return you to what is truly dependable: your heart. If you want a new apartment, add the phrase "so I can feel" and finish the phrase with whatever word your intuition supplies: "stability," perhaps, or "beauty," or "peace." And then, holding this feeling-word tenderly in your heart, as you would hold a birthday gift for a dear friend, tell yourself, "This is what I want for myself, above all." If you can wish yourself well with creativity and sincerity, you will find your wish has already been granted. It was granted long ago, in fact, at the very hour of your birth.

32. ∾ ONE-WORLD AWARENESS

My teacher likes to say: "Instead of trying to make a change, make a shift." You may have good reason for wanting to change your life, your relationships, or your government. But when you fixate on what you don't want, you create two divergent worlds: one where your ideals exist already fulfilled, the other where you actually live, with all your frustrations and resentments. And so you must practice one-world awareness. Just as the people with whom you disagree politically are not going to disappear any time soon, so too the parts of yourself that you dislike are not going to disappear any time soon, no matter how much you try to force them into submission. One world, like it or not. That doesn't mean you have to accept the status quo; on the contrary, the sooner you accept that you live in one world, the sooner you will have the momentum of that world on your side. So today, take a more gradual approach to your transformation. If you are trying to give up watching TV or eating junk food or having conversations that bring you down, try to do these things just a little less. And then feel the joy that comes from noticing your incremental progress and from understanding that big change comes from small shifts. The will of a nation can shift in a heartbeat, and your heart can shift in even less time than that.

33. ∾ FOLLOW THIS DAY

Question your desires. The world will tell you that desire is freedom, but desire is more like a stake in the ground to which the plant of your life is bound and guided by. At times, you may need a little structure, a little desire, to guide you, but be careful about growing according to the world's narrow measure, for the straightest branch is the first one cut down for timber. If you want to live and die free, be like a crooked tree that grows according to where the light is. When your mind insists you need more pleasure, more praise, more stuff, just tell yourself: "Let me follow this day where it wants to take me." Let your life grow strange and marvelous, more intricate, yet simpler than anything contained within the small range of ordinary desire.

34. ∾ DIGNITY IN DESIRE

The important thing is to find some dignity in desire. We can become fools chasing after what we think we want; we can also become fools trying to resist it. What brings us dignity is the ability to see desire in terms of cause and effect, for when we see clearly the steps and sacrifices necessary to attain what we want, we neither feel so threatened by our desires nor so enchanted by them. When we were young, we played at scavenger hunts: games in which the point of discovering one thing was to let it lead you to another. In those games, we neither rested content with attaining one object nor agonized about reaching the final goal, for we knew that the fun was in the finding. And it is this ability to play with desire, to see it not as an end in itself but as a series of clues leading to some greater treasure, that we must relearn as adults. So today, ask yourself what feeling your desires are pointing toward, and let the clues the outer world provides lead you inside, toward something you have understood before but have forgotten many times: your heart. Try not to judge your desires or believe in them too quickly, but let them educate you even as you educate them. If you are learning something, you are moving in the right direction.

35. ∾ HOW MUCH DO YOU REALLY NEED?

Ask the question, "How much do I really need?" and ask it of your mind as well as your body. For the conflicts of our world are caused as much by the unlimited need for status, praise, and self-righteousness, as by the need for oil or other material resources. And just as politics cannot be separated from habits of consumption, peace cannot be separated from habits of mind.

36. ∾ THE STORY THROUGH TO THE END

What the heart wants, above all, is to be free. People say, "I followed my heart and it got me into trouble," but they're not telling the whole story, just the opening chapters, in which our hero mistakes addiction for love, and reactivity for spontaneity. If you really want to follow your heart, you have to think the story through to the end. If you want something, ask yourself: "Where is this wanting taking me, and will I be more free when I get there?" Be careful not to judge yourself for having desires, for if you separate head from heart in that way, you will surely keep making the same mistakes. Think of your life not as a struggle to resist temptation, but as a deep longing for the open road, an unimpeded path of living on which you can walk at peace and at ease.

37. ∾ HOMING PIGEONS

How do you want to feel today? If that question sounds silly, it is only because we keep burying it beneath our endless plans for getting the *things* we think will make us feel something one day. But if you could see that your desires are like a flock of pigeons that always know how to find their way home if you just point them in the right direction and let them go, you would live your life with less worry. Fretting about how a desire will be fulfilled is like putting those birds in the trunk of your car and robbing them of their joy and their power. And so you must find the place where desire can be free: nowhere in the world around you, but in the inner sky of your body. Ask yourself today, "How do I want to feel?"

and see if you can let your body breathe in a way that brings fulfillment to that desire. What kind of breathing would make you feel more loved? More safe? More protected? More full of power or peace? Whatever you need, there is a breath that knows how to meet that need. And as you practice desire within you, your outer world will change too. You will see that everything is unraveling and tumbling and loosening its grip upon the world, not in order to plunge into some dark abyss, but for the pure thrill of taking flight through the air.

38. ∾ SOMEWHERE NEW

Some believers in reincarnation say that if you want something, you must once have had it, lost it, and now crave it again. Whether across many lifetimes or in this one, most desires are repetitions and cannot take us anywhere we haven't already been. So for today, ask yourself: "Where can I go that is truly new?" Live as close to the bone of this question as you can. For we are here just a short while, and are more than dogs who return to their own vomit, convinced they've found another meal.

39. ∾ LOVE OF WHAT IS REAL

Beauty does not come from having what we want, but from wanting what we already have. And what we have, in the end, is our actions—the way we relate to our experience. We have been taught the opposite, of course, mostly by people who wanted our money or our help in confirming their worst fears. But in reality, the beauty we have been taught to strive and compete for comes only from choosing and inhabiting life as it already is, from "love of what is real," as al-Ghazali put it. Look at all the human bodies, which are after all just sacks of blood and skin, and you will see that their beauty emerges only when people inhabit their forms completely, committing to their imperfections perfectly. And so we must learn to want what we already have: our intentions. Whatever happens to us, we have the ability to meet it with love, to strengthen that ability each and every day. So today, ask yourself: "What beauty can I bring to this moment?" There is beauty in how you choose to focus on your surroundings, beauty in the grace you bring to your movements, beauty in the kind thoughts you choose to think. Embrace these actions as passionately you would embrace a lover.

40. ∾ THE REAL GAMBLE

Take some risks in your life. The meaningful ones aren't found in chasing after more, but in looking for happiness in less. We have a longing for adventure, which we tend to associate with gain or pleasure or status, but the real gamble, the real adventure, lies in whether you will be able to find happiness apart from these things, in freedom from craving, clinging, and obsession. There is probably some road ahead that feels closed to you. You have been pushing forward for a long time and getting nowhere. Take a chance: stop pushing. Focus instead on some area of your life in which you feel genuine contentment, and ask yourself how that feeling registers in your body. Stay close to these sensations of contentment, and you will need neither roads nor maps to cross the cosmos.

41. ∾ STAY HUNGRY

Stay hungry. There is a kind of ambition that is good for you, one that expresses itself not in greed or brute force, but in the persistent questioning of life. Each morning, when you rise, ask yourself: "How can I let a little more sunlight through my window? How can I let more joy into my veins?" The noblest ambition is always paired with the greatest persistence. Guard against complacency, but also against impatience, for a question is only a question if you are willing to wait for an answer. Start with your breath. Let it be comfortable, but keep asking, "What kind of breathing would feel even better?" Don't try to make anything happen, just pose the question and watch as the limits of what you are capable of feeling expand, right there at your nostrils. Life never explains its boundaries to us, but it does answer all our questions, in its own time and its own tongue, a tongue all of us can learn.

42. ∽ LIFE MEETS YOU HALFWAY

Life will meet you halfway. Trees given water give back fruit, and the love you take is equal to the love you make. We know this on some level, yet what keeps us from believing in the deep reciprocity at the heart of all things is our habit of focusing on external actions instead of inner intentions. We think, *I did that for him, and look: he did nothing for me!* What we fail to see, beneath the surface of our efforts, are the "near enemies" that give our actions the opposite effect of what they seem to aim at. Good deeds born of self-pity, for example, only lead to feeling pitiable. Good deeds born of attachment lead to feeling helpless. Good deeds born of competition lead to feeling competed with. Good deeds born of indifference lead to living in an indifferent world. Our circumstances are not always fair, but on the level of intention, there is a law that always connects what we reap with what we sow. So today, pick an area of your life in which you feel you give more than you get, and put a little less effort into external action and a little more into the quality of your intention. If people are taking advantage of you, give them a little less of your time and energy, but give them more of your goodwill and compassion. And then watch: if you are truthful and observant, you will start to develop a deep conviction in your ability to shape your life by bringing love to each and every moment.

43. ∼ Love for No Reason at All

We are not alive in order to have relationships. We have relationships in order to remember why we are alive. We are here to find a higher love, one that serves no function greater than itself, not a social order or an economic order or the order of our own vanity. We do not come to love as interlocking parts of a machine, but as free and separate souls. And yet, the more clearly we understand that interdependence is not the final purpose of our existence, the better and more tenderly we end up getting along.

44. ∼ Every Journey Begins with a Goodbye

Every journey begins with a goodbye. If you feel frightened by the future, it may be that you are trying to carry the harbor with you on your voyage. Look into your life: there is a way of growth that is waiting for you to say goodbye to something else. People will tell you you can have it all, but their words are advertising, not encouragement, and are mostly designed to keep you pliable and unsatisfied. True contentment comes from seeing that the great thing you were meant to do depends on letting other things pass. While you can never rush your goodbyes, you can begin to practice them daily in the realm of your attention, by focusing on one thing at a time and learning to put all other thoughts to the side. For what you do with your attention is what you do with your life, and what you need most now is not violence toward the past, but the conviction that one small thing can in fact open up onto everything. And that is something you can begin to see today.

45. ∼ An Unexpected Step on the Stairs

The opening of the heart is not a metaphor. It is not an idea or a sentimental way of saying something else. The opening of your heart is something you can feel, as you would feel any felt sensation, right at the center of your chest. And it is in learning to feel love this way, rather than merely think about it, that we encounter the greatest surprise in life: that our hearts can be closed even when our minds are open to love. There will be times—perhaps with a friend whom you tried to forgive too soon, perhaps with yourself, whom you vowed to love without really understanding that vow—when the closing of your heart will awaken you, as a sleepwalker might be awoken by an unexpected step on the stairs. And at these moments, when the truth of your closed heart surprises you, you must learn to see that truth as a gift. You must push off of it, as a swimmer might push off the bottom of a lake, without resenting the fact that you still have more work to do in order to find real love. So today, try to keep your attention at the center of your chest, and ask yourself frequently: "How is my heart?" Notice not just the expansions, but the contractions too. For the irony is this: as soon as you accept yourself as you actually are, a person in whom love does not flow easily sometimes, the cramped muscle of your heart will release and begin to open.

46. ∾ MEMORIES OF THE FUTURE

Faith is not a light that gets suddenly switched on, nor does it come from checking your brain at the door of some church or organization. Faith is the growing, gradual realization that what you let remain in your heart today is what will still be there tomorrow. If you are afraid of living now, you will still be afraid even when you meet with good fortune. If you are generous now, you will still feel you have plenty even when times are tough. And when you see that what connects you to the life you want is not your incessant planning but the qualities of mind you cultivate, you will start to have faith in your ability to live as you choose. So today, try to think of faith as cause and effect. Help someone out, forgive those who have hurt you, practice patience toward all that is difficult in your life — but above all, understand that what you are feeling in the present is a memory of the future, and though the details still are hazy, your heart already sees what your eyes cannot.

47. ∾ Investing in the Present

What you have to give to this life, above all, is your care. You have a little money, a little time, a little talent, and it's good to try each day to stretch the limits of these things with your generosity. But in the end, these resources are limited by conditions you can't control. What you can control is whether you bring your wholehearted attention to whatever you are doing right now, and whether you understand the power contained in that simple act. In the seventeenth century, economists believed that trading with foreign countries would make a nation poor, but we know now that global investments, done wisely, can lead to greater wealth for all. The economy of your heart is the same: the more you invest in the present moment and all that it contains, the more you will find you have to give. So today, as often as you can remember, remind yourself, What I'm doing right now is important. Whether you are standing on line in a store, listening to a family member prattle on, or just watching leaves blow down the street, try to give your breath and your heart to what is happening. You are in the right place to change your life.

48. ∾ Leaning Too Far over the Balcony

If you want to feel safe and protected in this life, you must learn not to lean so far into the future. We are always leaning forward, across our relationships and careers, trying to touch what is coming next. We are like children leaning over a fragile balcony railing, not realizing that these things cannot support us, not realizing that all we will ever touch in this way is the free fall of time. No matter what you think is coming at you today, remind yourself that the way forward lies in taking a step back from the edge of all your striving until you can connect with your heart and its deeper wish for happiness. Close your eyes. Picture yourself as a child, at a moment when you were happy. Picture yourself smiling or playing or running free. And then remind yourself that the happiness you felt then is the same happiness available to you now — a happiness that is always there and your birthright. And as you go out into the world, reflect on what success is, what it really looks and feels like to you. And perhaps you will find that it is not found in grasping after an attainment or an image, but in slowly, gradually, letting these things go.

49. ∾ VISIONS OF THE FUTURE

How much of a vision of the future do you need? Visions can be inspiring, but they can be storehouses of anxiety and delusion too. And just as a long life is not necessarily better than a short one, a long view is not necessarily wiser than seeing clearly what you are doing right now. In reality, we need both a long and a short view, for as the Buddha said, a man traveling to a distant city needs to know not only the way, but also whether he's currently on the right road. In the same way, the question is not simply whether you will find happiness in this life, but also, when you do, whether you will have the strength of mind to know it fully. Will you be like a passenger who glimpses an ocean for a moment through the window of a train, or like a swimmer in the sea, fully immersed in and carried by what you love? Start developing strength of mind today, for it will not come more easily with age. Focus on your breath, your body, or any part of your experience that feels good, but practice staying, staying, staying with just one thing. This is how you see infinity in a grain of sand. This is how you see the future right here in the present.

50. ∾ WELL MAY THE WORLD GO, WHEN I'M FAR AWAY

Try not to confuse love with time. Making time for what you love is an important and beautiful practice, but in the end, you will never have enough time for what you love, nor will you be able to squeeze the intensity of all you feel into a schedule or the brief span of your life. And so, you must learn a different kind of loyalty—to things as they are: brief, tender, and incomplete. Recall the words of that old folk song, "Well may the world go, when I'm far away," even as you draw nearer to what is dear to your heart. At first, it may be hard to love others, to love this world, with yourself taken out of the picture. And yet, the more you can develop this ability to love from a distance, to love from the perspective of death, the larger the space of every moment will become, till you find that time gives way to infinity and within the constraints of a single touch or a single breath, there is somehow enough time to feel it all completely.

51. ∾ MINDFULNESS MEANS REMEMBERING WHAT MATTERS

In the end, your happiness is determined not by the experiences you have, but by your ability to remember and act upon something that has always been right in front of you: love. On a cosmic level, if space and time are infinite, then not only have you already been everybody else before, but you have also already had all the experiences: you have won and lost everything, been desired and rejected by everyone, found and forgot the god you hoped to meet in church or on that ayahuasca journey next weekend. All of this has happened to you infinite times. But what have these experiences taught you, other than the fact that no amount of experience can ever make you remember what is important? In the middle of paradise, you can still be alone with your tormented thoughts; in the middle of hell, you can still remember your blessings. Your remembrance, unlike your experience, is free and voluntary. It depends on you, and you can depend on it. So today, do your best to keep what matters in mind: the love you have for yourself, your goodwill for others, and the breath at your nostrils that sustains you. And then act on these remembrances, for you cannot help but to act, whether mindfully or mindlessly. You do not have to climb a high mountain or turn some great tide. You only have to learn the gentle art of looking up from whatever you are lost in and asking yourself: "What is it that I have forgotten? What message did I come here to deliver?"

52. ∾ OLD MOVIE REELS

It can take a long time to understand that our tortured thoughts about love are not love, but something else entirely. They are old movie reels, perhaps, projected on the walls of our minds, whose characters cannot hear us and whose endings are all the same, no matter how we view them. It can take a long time to understand that the work of love does not consist of directing or rewriting anything, but of learning to switch off the projector and wait in darkness for something still invisible, yet already more true, to come. It can take a long time, but if we learn to wait, we will have all the real love in the world to gain, and much misery to lose.

53. ∾ THE OTHER SIDE OF DISAPPOINTMENT

True love begins on the other side of disappointment. Until a person has let you down and yet you see his goodness anyway, until you understand the absurdity of trying to perfect your brief relationships in the face of death, you do not really love but only chase after what is easy. People are going to fail you, and you must treat their failures as an opportunity to work through your own disappointments and to find a love that does not break even when your ideals do. And the same is true of the love you have for yourself. We tend to think of self-love as pride or satisfaction in ourselves, but really it is the ability to show up for ourselves in spite of all the ways we have been disappointments to ourselves. So today, take some time to reflect on the ways you have let yourself down: the poor treatment you have given your body, the poor treatment you have given your mind with all your thoughts of self-criticism, the poor treatment you have given your words by failing to be true to them. And then, in spite of all these disappointments, see if you can think to yourself, softly and silently: *I forgive myself. For all the ways I've hurt myself, knowingly or unknowingly, I hold myself in kindness and mercy.* You will know you are on the right track when you feel not pride but relief. Relief that, after all these years, you are still on your own side. Relief that, after everything you have failed to do or become, you are still able to hold yourself in unconditional love.

54. ꙮ BLOOD ON YOUR HANDS

Love is not always a matter of making things right. It's good to help where you can, but we are too dependent on the idea that love brings resolution to all things. Imagine for a moment that you woke one morning to find you'd killed someone by accident. How would you move forward in your life with love? Would you sink in guilt or denial, or would you find another way? When you look soberly at the limits of your ability to fix circumstances, to change what has been done, you begin to understand that true love exists in the heart—that is, in a place whose value lies not in being able to control this uncontrollable world, but in being apart from and in spite of that world. So the next time someone is yelling at you over something petty or insignificant, maybe you don't have to yell back or defend yourself. Maybe you can just love, love with all your heart, and in time those around you will glimpse the other life that lies within this one.

55. ∾ You Don't Need to Deserve Anything

It's good to believe you deserve love. But it's even better to believe you don't need to deserve anything anymore. Those childhood days, when life seemed like a test for something else, are gone now. Don't waste your remaining time trying to earn what is free, or prove what comes from letting go of proving.

56. ∾ Exhausted by Guilt

The greatest tragedy is to be too exhausted by guilt to be able to love. Your mind will tell you that you have to carry days and nights of regret on your back, but your heart knows that true repentance only requires a single moment of clarity. If you have hurt someone, apologize, but make your apology a waterwheel that turns the energy of sorrow back out into the world as sympathy and goodwill. Picture the person you have hurt happy or at peace, and if that is too much for you, then just be kind to the next person who crosses your path. If your actions lead to suffering, see them for what they are, but don't lie down and let yourself be battered by waves of remorse. Turn, keep turning, with the river rushing through you, and empty yourself of anything that love cannot flow through.

57. ∾ A War Waged on the Past

Old humiliations drive us more than we admit. So much of what we call love is a war waged on the past. And yet, the past never submits. To live without regret you have to do more than accomplish great things. You have to become sensitive to the undertow of shame that drags you through this life, and learn how to get out from its current. We carry shame for what we've done; we carry it because it gives us an illusion of control over what has already happened. A part of us thinks: *If I should have done more, that means there was more that could have been done.* And so our struggles multiply, and the many-headed hydra of ambition grows harder to subdue. But in the midst of all this there is the breath, which asks nothing of you, and demands no apology for what has come before. Stay there and rest. There is less to do than you think.

58. ∾ LOVE MAKES US GROW AND GROW BEYOND EACH OTHER

When relationships change, we often think, *I didn't love well enough.* We forget that love is itself the cause of change, that the coming together of two people produces an expansion whose final limit and direction can never be known in advance. To love is to grow together but also beyond each other, like two trees planted close whose trunks lean on one another, but whose branches seek their own light in different parts of the sky. This is the truth of our separateness, which the thinking mind, with its labels of "breaking up" and "getting back together," can never really grasp. But the heart understands that separateness co-exists with togetherness, aloneness with community, and so on—and this is why we must develop our hearts, not just our relationships, in order to be happy. So today, put your hand on your heart and picture a few moments in your life when you were truly happy and free. And then reflect that the happiness you felt then is the same happiness you feel even now. Let memories course through you like water, and remind yourself that you yourself are a river: present in a form that will never come again, yet still flowing on, without beginning or end.

59. ∾ A CAR WITHOUT BRAKES

It isn't true that love lets you down. Bitterness will let you down, that's for sure, but we rarely see the enormous faith we place in our own resentments. Every day, when things don't go our way, we harbor a secret hope that if we hate them enough they will change.

And resentment is waiting for us, like a car without brakes, to carry us forward in our wild pursuit of happiness. And when we hit the telephone pole, we think: *How could love let this happen?* But no one ever asked us to get in the car. We do this all by ourselves.

60. ∞ ASHAMED OF LOVE

It can take a while to separate love from shame. We often think we stand for love because we support marriage equality or share inspiring quotes on the Internet, but the roots of shame run far deeper than politics or opinions. Right now, there are many things that bring you joy that you are still apologizing for: friends or lovers that don't meet the approval of those around you, passions that don't make for exciting stories at family gatherings, ways of living that don't fit the picture you had of yourself when you were younger. The truth is that you will always feel some shame in love until you start to believe, moment by moment, in your ability to know for yourself what truly makes you happy. And to do that, you have to strengthen your awareness, as you would strengthen any muscle—through practice. Ask yourself, "What really feels good right now . . . in my life, in my body, in my breath?" Practice with these little things, for shame is not an enemy you can defeat all at once on an open field. You win only by solidifying the walls of your mindfulness so that, no matter what people say or think, you hear nothing but the beating of your own heart.

61. ∞ MOST PROBLEMS ARE ONE PROBLEM

If you have a problem in one area of your life, you are probably already practicing the solution in another. If you have trouble with money, maybe love can teach you what it means to be of worth. If you have trouble with love, maybe money can teach you what it means to invest wisely. Most skills in life are transferable, because most problems are one problem: that we try to fight our experience rather than learn from it. So today, when you find yourself struggling, remember your skills. You have already learned so much. There are many ways to lay down a sword.

62. ∾ FINDING OUT

You might think it's hard to be present because there's so much on your mind right now, but the opposite is true: you keep so much on your mind to avoid being present. For you would rather suffer a thousand anxieties than face the fear that, stripped of all your distractions, you are really no one, unworthy of love. Like a teenager so scared of rejection that he never gets to find out that the girl he yearns for secretly yearns for him in return, your fear of finding out who you are without all your thoughts, plans, and activities also keeps you from discovering the great love that is waiting for you right here in the present moment. And that is why, today and every day, you must start to take some risks. Ride the train without a book in front of you or music in your ears. Walk down the street without thinking about the future. Give yourself to raw experience wherever you can. Do not see these as acts of deprivation, but as mustering up enough courage to make contact with the beloved. For there is another life—your true life—waiting in the present moment for you to approach. It does not judge you or ask you where you've been. It simply waits. Let it let you in.

63. ∾ LIVE CLOSE TO THE GROUND

Try not to confuse separation with abandonment. We are all separating from one another, the way boughs on a tree grow in different directions, and even if you never experience a "breakup" in the common sense of that word, the love you find in this life will always contain separation. For love makes us grow and grow beyond each other: it waters our common roots and also parts the branches of our lives. But none of this should persuade you that you have been forsaken, for you carry forever all the love you have ever felt, regardless of labels or appearances. Lao Tzu said that a wise man lives close to the ground, and this is true also of how we see love. Will we obsess about the ways our lives may diverge in the future, or will we see the timeless nature of the heart in which our roots are joined? So today, picture yourself at a moment in your life when you felt happy and loved. Perhaps you are smiling or resting or playing. And then see if you can feel right now the love that you felt then. See if you can understand that it is still here, always. See if you can understand that your access to it depends upon your focus, not upon external conditions. When you have seen all that, you will know that you are the only person who could ever abandon you.

64. ∾ PUTTING OUT FIRE WITH GASOLINE

It is not jealousy but fear of jealousy that does us harm. Jealousy is a flame that dies out on its own, but not wanting it to arise is like trying to put out fire with gasoline. We hurt each other most when we don't believe we can survive our own insecurities. And so we must always remember that we are not less for having difficult emotions, but greater than the difficult emotions we have. The next time you find yourself getting jealous, tell yourself, "Good, that means I'm alive. That means I care." And then, instead of lashing out at the other person or beating yourself up for not being perfectly composed, try to view your jealousy as a parent might view a child having a tantrum. What is my jealousy really asking for, beyond all the rage and drama? Give it your love, give it your understanding, but most of all, give it space. It will not destroy you. In fact, it is looking to you for guidance.

65. ∾ You Are Grown Now

You may feel abandoned, but you cannot be abandoned. Only a child, whose survival depends on a fixed point of love, can be abandoned. You are grown now, and have what it takes to find sustenance in everything and everyone you meet. You have the ability to grow in yourself the qualities you most desire, and to behold how life mirrors these in the others who cross your horizon. You are no longer a shape being drawn, but the hand that holds the pen. So while you will feel loss at times, and disappointment too, you can never be abandoned. You have survived the great scream of childhood. Surely you can live well among the echoes now.

66. ∾ Continuing Education

Spiritual practices are often substitutes for parental approval: it makes us feel accepted to walk a path others have said is good. But what will bring us happiness when graduation day is over? At some point, we have to start learning from the darker regions of our lives, those parts we've had trouble educating and respecting. In the midst of these difficulties, we have to become the good parents we have always yearned for. It's true: you find your feet only where life last knocked you down. Redemption doesn't happen in another person's eyes, or under any other circumstances than the ones you're struggling with right now.

67. ∾ As You Actually Are

Love yourself, not just the idea of yourself. We all know those relationships in which one person only loves the idea of the other. You can spot them from far off by the anxious way one of the people is looking around for an escape whenever the other doesn't behave in accordance with some ideal of beauty, intelligence, or success. But that's how we love ourselves most of the time. One moment, we think, I really am beautiful, smart, and successful, and the next, when something contradicts that idea, we start looking for something else—an identity, a distraction, a spiritual technique, like someone embarrassed to be seen out in public with an old high school friend. That isn't real love. In real love, there is an awareness of each moment's singularity and the sense that we have just one life to live and have decided to place our bets on the beloved, for better or worse, for richer or poorer, in sickness and in health. So today, try to love yourself as you actually are: disappointing sometimes, imperfect always, but the one you have chosen to walk this life with.

68. ❧ LOVE NEVER DIES A NATURAL DEATH

Try to see the difference between doing something perfectly and doing it well. We accept the idea of gradual mastery when it comes to playing the piano or shooting a basket, but when it comes to love and happiness, we think of these things as bolts of lightning that either strike or miss us, and we are extremely resistant to the idea that skill might be involved. Until we see, as Anaïs Nin put it, that "love never dies a natural death. It dies because we don't know how to replenish its source," we will always feel depleted and unlucky, no matter how wonderful the people around us are. Moment by moment, we replenish love through our intentions and our willingness to believe that every action counts. So today, try to feel that though you are imperfect and though the shape of your relationships is often beyond your control, your ability to love and feel loved is not. Bring your attention to your heart and say the words until you can feel them: "Let me try to love well." There is no test, no external standard, and yet, there is this urge to love better, to love deeper, that you cannot deny any more than you can keep the springtime from coming.

69. ∾ An Exit Is Also an Entrance

You aren't obligated to work on every relationship. Let the wrong ones out. But before you open a door, ask yourself what else might come through it. For every exit doubles as an entrance, and it is to see this that we must stay longer with what is difficult.

70. ∾ Strategy Is the Death of Love

Strategy is the death of love. We work so hard to force our feelings into final conclusions, forgetting that love is not a feeling or a conclusion, but the state of being right in time with wherever you are, whomever you are with. Love, unlike infatuation, is a balance of passion and patience, a momentum that neither pushes forward nor stands still. So when you feel you are losing love, when you fear something rare and precious is slipping away, remind yourself that you are right where you need to be to be right in time. Don't try to trick love into standing naked before you, like those folktales in which a man steals a maiden's clothes while she is bathing. Look beyond the man and the maiden toward the river of each moment, and seek within it the soft current that carries you to true love. Look around you and ask, "What is beautiful about this moment?" If you look with fresh eyes at the color of paint on the wall or the smile on a passing stranger's face or even the powerful longing within you, stripped of all its usual stories, you will find that love is neither leaving nor arriving. Without plans or projections, it is simply here, right in time.

71. ∾ Don't Fall Asleep in the Garden

Travel wherever you like in your mind, but don't fall asleep at the wheel. There is a great difference between active imagination and passive fantasy. The thinking mind is like a magic garden we read about in fairy tales, filled with all sorts of wondrous things, but also visited by malevolent spirits. As we walk through the garden, we become so enchanted by the objects we find that rather than taking what we need and leaving in haste, we lie down in dangerous pastures and drift off. And as we sleep, we become afflicted: fantasies about sex turn to fears of not being desirable enough; fantasies about fame turn to fears of being insignificant. And so you must learn to interrupt your daydreams and ask yourself, "Why am I here? What was I searching for? Is any of this useful?" If you look, you will see that your thoughts about sex often disguise a deeper longing for connection or comfort or self-expression; your thoughts about fame often disguise a deeper longing for spontaneity or creativity or ease. Take these deeper desires seriously, and don't waste your time worrying about whether sex or fame or money or pleasures are in themselves good or bad. Just remind yourself that you want to be well. Between worlds of illusion and worlds of boredom, you want to live in a world where imagination and reality are one.

72. ∾ THE ARCHER'S GAZE

Try to focus on your inner intentions, not just your external actions, as you go through this day. You may have lots of opinions about what you should be doing with your life: changing jobs, meditating more, eating this, thinking that. But just as the path of an arrow follows an archer's gaze, not the strength of his bow, so too all these outer actions, however powerful, will miss their target if you don't learn how to aim first. Moment by moment, you are either aiming at love or something else—greed, hatred, delusion—and a good indicator of what you're aiming at is how you feel. If you are "taking care" of your life in a way that feels joyless, you probably aren't taking such good care. We move forward not just by what we do, but how we do it, and why. So today, when the old desire to change your life arises, insert the phrase, "because I want to feel" into your thoughts: "I want to work harder because I want to feel a sense of purpose and accomplishment," "I want to eat better because I want to feel ease and wellbeing in my body," etc. And beyond the content of your words, listen to the sound of your thoughts, and make up your mind that, before all else, you will only listen to an opinion if it can adopt a friendly tone of voice.

73. ∾ THE COMPATIBILITY TRAP

In the end, the strength of any relationship comes from intention, not compatibility. It's nice to be around people who make it easy for you to be your best self, but there are limits to that passive way of living. Anyone worth having in your life is going to bring out the worst in you at times, and at those moments when you find compatibility breaking down, it is your intention that will determine the relationship and your life with others. Sometimes, in the company of someone you desperately want to connect with, you will have to be alone with your thoughts of goodwill for that person. Sometimes you will have to change the subject, or dodge what's being thrown at you, or refuse to see the worst in the other person even when that person wants you to. Love means keeping your eye on the ball no matter what, not just waiting for a soft pitch. So today, make it a practice to pause before you react to what seems incompatible with what you want, and use the pause to set a heartfelt intention of love or compassion. Ask yourself, "What do I want to be creating here?" For you are creating, whether or not you do so consciously. Don't worry about how the relationship looks on the outside, or whether the pieces fit together with ease or difficulty. The pieces of a good life don't have to go together. If you love them, they will grow together.

74. ∾ How You Care for Anything Is How You Care for Everything

Wish all people well, without exception, and guard against the idea that some are more deserving of your goodwill than others. If you see someone prospering, wish her joy in what she has, for tomorrow she may have nothing but the kindness you have shown her. If you see someone being cruel, wish her freedom from suffering, for tomorrow she may feel the pain of his mistakes and need your compassion to turn his life around. None of us has an aerial view of the road ahead, nor a complete map of cause and effect, and so there is a dishonesty at the heart of any judgment about who is "worthy" of a particular blessing. All we have, at any given moment, is the compass of our own goodwill, which simply tells us the next right step to take. Time and energy for helping others may be scarce, but goodwill costs you nothing and is always available. So try to see this day as an opportunity to bring an attitude of care to what lies before you, imperfect though it may be. How you care for anything is in a sense how you care for everything. So don't wait for the world to overcome its limitations in order to make your goodwill limitless.

75. ∾ What Will I Become?

Of all the pressing questions, there is really only one: If I keep thinking the way I think right now, in time what will I become?

76. ∾ Cathedral on a Cracked Foundation

Be careful about seeing your life as a series of sacrifices. There will always be people who say that you have to do or be what feels wrong in order to live right. Anyone can tell you that if you push hard enough against a wall it will one day turn into a door. But there are many things in life that feel hard precisely because they are dead ends, and you must guard against the ego's desire to rise to every challenge, for some challenges are not worth rising to. You will know an endeavor is worth your time when it requires joyful persistence, not martyrdom, when what is difficult about it are the patience and faith it demands, not pain and struggle. For the true path is good in the beginning, good in the middle, and good in the end, so keep your standards high and don't settle for what your heart knows not to be true, lest you waste your life building a cathedral on a cracked foundation.

77. ❧ CHEWING YOUR OWN FOOD

You are listening to yourself. There is no idea or authority in this world more persuasive than the voices in your own head. And so it is that you are totally free and also totally responsible for your own happiness. We keep waiting for the world to show us its goodness, like baby birds waiting for their parents to chew their food for them. We want a happiness that is pre-digested. But we must learn to chew our own food, to extract goodness from the present moment, whether or not that moment is pleasant. The key is to see the present moment not as an experience, but as a learning experience. Today, when things get challenging, remember to ask yourself, "What can I learn here?" Instead of furiously trying to run the engine of your joy, try taking that engine apart to see how it actually works. Forget your false positivity and all that "It's all good" talk. It isn't all good. But it all contains good. And in that difference is the secret of growth.

78. ❧ DON'T MOVE IN WITH YOUR FIRST CONCLUSION

Judging your own thoughts is a bit like judging the people you date: if a thought wants all your attention right away, no matter how attractive it is, it's probably crazy. This is especially true for self-criticism, which tends to come on strong in both its urgency and persuasiveness. But it's not so much that things and people are persuasive, it's that we persuade ourselves about them, especially when we feel lonely or desperate. So if you want to let the right kinds of criticism in, you first have to understand the sense of panic inside you that makes you want to move in with the first conclusion that comes your way. You can soften that panic by reflecting on your own kindness and generosity and the fact that you have a goodness that exists whether or not you find solutions to all your problems. As for your promising suitors, thank them and tell them to come back next week. Any thought worth thinking can wait.

79. ∿ DEADLINES FOR DAYDREAMS

Don't confuse a creative life with a life lost in thought. The difference is this: the ability to give your daydreams some deadlines. Most daydreams are like a corrupt charity that promises all sorts of good and then disappears with your money. A thought about being with this partner or getting that opportunity may have some goodness in it, but if you look closely, you will see that the first moments of a fantasy are nearly always followed by long periods of frustration over not yet having what you want—frustration that leads to self-doubt and to forgetting the joy that gave birth to your dream in the first place. So if you're going to give a dream your time and resources, try to hold it accountable. Tell whatever thought arises, "You have five breaths to prove yourself." If a thought has value, after five breaths it should make you feel more relaxed, more alive, and more free to put your attention wherever you choose. But if after five breaths, the thought has begun to boss you around, it's time to change the channel. "In dreams begin responsibilities," Yeats wrote. And responsibility is not just a matter of scheduling or planning or making things happen, but of seeing the ship of your mind clearly, and remembering that you are not a passenger on it, but the captain of it.

80. ∾ HELICOPTER PARENTS

What is meditation? It is the art of learning to watch over your life without becoming overly involved in it. Your life, like your children, has been entrusted to your care. But like a child, your life has its own destiny: it will grow and change in ways you cannot control. And like a child, your life will also leave you one day. So you have to learn how to keep an eye on your own growth without becoming like those "helicopter parents" who are hyper-present yet emotionally absent, constantly scheduling this or that activity out of the fear they haven't done enough. It is good to work on yourself, but it is even better to ask the question often, "How much do I have to do and how much can I just leave alone?" My teacher often says that it only takes a moment for the heart to understand suffering: anything longer is just over-complication. So today, take a look at the amount of time you spend thinking about your self-improvement. Is this time you are spending out of love for yourself, or are you just in the habit, like much of our news media, of picking the most disturbing conflict and focusing your camera on it? This is meditation: not learning to sit like a statue, but learning to do what needs to be done and then resting in gratitude.

81. ∾ THE FOG OF FEELING UNHEARD

We so often walk in a fog of feeling unheard that we are surprised sometimes to find how deeply our speech can penetrate others. Knowing this, we should live as though we are constantly being listened to, for in fact, we are: In each of us, there is one who hears everything. In each of us, there is one who, like a child, may not seem to understand, but who is daily growing into the shape of our words.

82. ∾ INFINITE ECHOES

Try to speak as though your words would echo back to you for-ever, as though everything you ever uttered would be preserved and repeated again and again. We think words fade into the air, and our whole culture—from our political debates to the comments sec-tion of YouTube—is designed to convince us of the insignificance of language, to convince us that though we may have a voice in the short term, we don't really have a voice in the long term. But if we understood that words are seeds we throw ahead of us—they become habits of mind, which become consciousness, which become the world we build and then inherit—we would speak much differently. So today, pick an area of your life in which you tend to use words carelessly and ask yourself, "What kind of a world do I want to live in?" If someone has been saying hurtful things to you, remember that your response has far more power to shape your future than do that person's remarks. Take yourself seriously. You have a voice. Use it to create something beautiful.

83. ∾ SPEAK WITH GRACE

If you want to rediscover the freshness and vitality of your life, take good care of the words you use. People often say, "That's just talk. We want change!" But where do you think real change comes from, if not the words by which you guide and shape your actions, which guide and shape your life? And where do you think boredom and stagnation come from, if not a mind that can no longer rely on words to navigate and penetrate experience? The world appears as dead or as alive, as empty or as full, as the truth of the words you use. So make it a practice, each and every day, to mean what you say. That means, first of all, not telling lies, but it also means having a felt sense of your words: how they feel as they leave your lips and fall upon ears. When you are with family or friends or by yourself in silence, let the tone of your voice be deliberate, heartfelt, and even musical. Speak with grace. Life can be tragic, life can be comical, but when you mean what you say, life is always alive.

84. ∾ A Conversation Needs a Roof

Make it a practice of love to learn how to end conversations, even with those you are close to. Just as a house needs a roof, love needs a limit to keep it safe and protected. It can be just as challenging to find affection in the ending of words as it is to find peace in the death of our bodies, but we have what it takes to develop both these skills, and in fact they both are related. So in the middle of any interaction today, ask yourself: "How can I close this circle with kindness?" We are used to words ending only with a trauma, with the slamming of a door or the violence of some deliberate distraction, but we can end with love too: with a smile, a word of appreciation, and above all, the willingness to let die all that is not essential between us.

85. ∾ Friendship

Friendship is the truest form of love. We are tribal beings, sexual beings, beings of flesh and hunger—and yet, whom we choose apart from biology and chemistry reflects who we are at our most free. Our families and lovers are blessings, of course, but we will only be happy in these areas of our lives to the extent that we discover in them the qualities of true friendship: respect, freedom, and a sense of separateness within our togetherness. For at the end of the day, our friends have their own lives. When they say goodbye, they teach us what society, with its delusions of possession, cannot. So take some time each day to reflect on your friends, to develop gratitude for them, but also wisdom about the possibilities of living they have shown you. Call them to mind, one by one, and try to feel the happiness you have found through them. Hold on to this feeling tightly; try not to forget it. It is more dependable than your best-laid plan, and will be your victory when everything else has come and gone.

86. ∾ LOVE IS NOT A FEELING

Love is not a feeling. Pleasant feelings are like any other pleasures: fragile, addictive, and in need of being defended. Our hearts are capable of something greater. We are more than dogs that bark at those who try to take our bones.

87. ∾ PACE YOURSELF

Love, like physical exercise, is in many ways a matter of pacing. Your emotions, like your heart rate, are healthiest when they remain just slightly elevated over a longer period of time, rather than pushed into extreme peaks followed by long periods of dullness and inactivity. Our trouble is that we think love is an experience—a rendezvous with a stranger, a honeymoon in France, a vision in the desert, a new house, a commitment—and because we spend most of our lives passively waiting for these experiences to happen, when they actually do, they traumatize us, just as someone who hasn't run in months will pull a muscle if she tries to sprint all at once. The ideal for the heart, as for the body, is a soft perpetual motion, a gentle connection with love and joy at every moment and in every situation. To accomplish this, realize that you don't need to rest the way you think you do. Inexperienced runners may come to a complete stop after every lap, but experienced runners know that it's better to soften the pace and keep moving forward, albeit more slowly. In the same way, when you're feeling empty of love and light, don't let go of your mind completely and spiral down into darkness. Focus instead on the little things that make you feel alive, things you merely like or that are merely nice. Think of your bad days and bad moods not as falling down, but as slowing down, and use these opportunities to reconnect with the secret sources of strength within you.

88. ∾ We Were Together, I Forget the Rest

The secret to patience is communion with yourself. When you were a teenager, riding in a car with your parents for just a few minutes may have felt like torture. And yet, on a road trip with friends, you never thought to ask, "Are we there yet?" for you knew that every moment was an opportunity to connect. The same is true of everything you are impatient about right now: your career, your love life, your own spiritual development. In all of these, your impatience is a sign that you have not yet connected with some part of yourself. So try to think of your frustrations as though they belong to someone you love. Be with them with the same compassion you would feel sitting across the table from a friend sharing his struggles with you. Whether you are on line at a post office or dealing with some kind of rejection, remind yourself, "This is an opportunity for me to connect." Bring your awareness to your heart and listen to your unfulfilled needs without judging or trying to fix them. Don't ask when it will all be over, for it will all be over soon enough. Just try to live so that if someone were to ask you at the end of your life, "Did you find success?" you could answer, in the words of Walt Whitman: "We were together—All else has long been forgotten by me."

89. ∾ Holes in the Bucket

Love is wisdom, not just affection. Affection is like the rain, which falls on all people alike, and if you hold out your bucket, you will get your share in time. The problem isn't lack of water, but the holes in your awareness through which affection keeps escaping. And so it is wisdom that you need in order to see where you are leaking and to patch what has been ruptured. To find wisdom, you need the company of wise beings—not just those who flatter you with money, power, pleasure, or praise, but those who, without judgment or pity, are willing to put their fingers on your wounds and heal you with kind attention. Wise beings are all around you, but you will know them only when you start to see all people with wisdom, to see in them an inherent ability to be happy, regardless of circumstances. So today, with everyone you meet, think to yourself, *There is enough love for you. You are enough love.* Your mind might protest that this person has been broken or damaged beyond repair, but that isn't true. Wisdom sees wholeness even where there are cracks, and in emptiness, a readiness to be full.

90. ∾ TRUE FRIENDS
True friends remind us that we have what it takes to meet impermanence with joy. In their company, our hearts grow feet and run like children toward the vanishing horizon.

91. ∾ THERE IS NO LOVE, ONLY PROOF OF LOVE
Take a walk today, and imagine, for a moment, that every person, tree, or building you pass is on your side, that each one is supporting you in your search for happiness. If that thought seems crazy, ask yourself: "How do I know the limits of the world that sustains me?" If you look at life this way, you realize something important: The experience of being loved always begins in the mind. The mind that is not attuned to love can never feel loved, while the mind that is can feel loved from every direction. So begin thoughts of goodwill for yourself. Wish yourself happiness, safety, health, ease of being. Try to feel these qualities somewhere in your body, somewhere where the physical sensations remind you that love is real. The point is not to guess at pretty notions, but to test the boundaries of your heart till you are sure there are none. The French say, "There is no love,

only proof of love." Perhaps the deeper meaning of that proverb is this: it is only by starting with goodwill for yourself that you will find assurance that there is a universal love that has been patiently waiting for you.

92. ∾ As Though You Would Live Forever

Forget about living each day as though it were your last. Try to live instead as though you live forever, as though nothing you do will ever be forgotten, as though everything that happens to you—the good, the bad, the beautiful, the brutal—is a page in the story of the life you want to live. When bombs go off in cities around the world, it is right to grieve, but do not let your grief distract you from the indestructible fertility at the heart of all life. Today, like every other day, the seeds you sow will ripen, the love you care for will flourish, and the stories you tell will become the story of your life. The struggle takes place in your awareness as much as on city streets or foreign soil. So keep careful watch over your mind, over the story you are telling, and do not let yourself become jaded by the ghosts of your former idealism. For we were never promised a garden, you know. We lived there once, perhaps, and we will live there again when we learn how to make things grow.

93. ∾ One Last Ride

Love—real love—is what prepares us to leave this life. If you've ever taken a child to a carousel, you know how quickly the child learns the words, "One last time!" and how quickly you learn that there never is one last time, not in any natural sense, for as long as the merry-go-round keeps turning, desire for it is never really satisfied, only temporarily subdued. And it is the same with your life: there is no last ride or last word or las t experience that could ever bring your existence to completion. The pain of your attachment to living is the same whether you go on a long time or a short time, whether you go down in a blaze of glory or die a slow, protracted death. And yet, there is love. Love not only comforts us, but teaches us that we can be happy as we are leaving this life. Love teaches, not by tearing us from life or moving us to cling to it more tightly, but in the way that a loving parent might say, "Yes, love, we can ride one more time, but only if we start getting ready to go." So today, even as you appreciate your life, keep asking yourself what it would take to get you ready to leave it. Are the relationships and pleasures you associate with love leading you to realize that this one life is enough, or are these things whipping up a desire in you for more and more rides around the same circle? You don't have as much time as you think. The sun is setting, and something is holding your hand, trying to lead you home.

APPRECIATION

(*summer*)

94. ᦰ Gratitude Is the Main Event

We are in the habit of seeing gratitude the way we did as children: when someone gave us something sweet, our parents said, "Now say thank you." In other words, we see gratitude as a way of getting permission to indulge in the candy we're eating. To really grow up, we must realize that all our candy—our pleasure, success, money, praise—is impermanent and unsatisfactory. Our gratitude is therefore not a preliminary to anything else; it is the main event, in which life's true excitement reveals itself. So the next time you feel uninspired or stuck in a rut, take some time to count your blessings. Make sure to go beyond focusing on jobs and relationships to the inner blessings that make these outer things worthwhile. Relationships, for example, are only worthwhile if they teach you how to open your heart. Jobs are only worthwhile if they teach you how to take care of yourself happily. And then, once you have developed gratitude, ask yourself what the future might hold that you are genuinely excited about. You may be amazed to find that the list is endless.

95. ᦰ Before You Jump out of Bed

So much depends upon the first few moments of the morning. We are used to seeing life through our rigid routines—eating right, working out, doing formal practices of meditation or yoga—that we forget that none of these structured activities has as much power to affect the rest of the day as do the first thoughts we think upon waking. Like thoughts attract like thoughts, and so the earlier in the day we think a thought, the more power it has to color all the others that follow. If we start with anxieties, complaints, and doubts, these are what we will likely find in later activities we might otherwise have benefitted from. So make it a practice not to leave your bed, not even to move, till you have found a few good thoughts to think, if only for a minute. Ajaan Mun used to start each day by spreading thoughts of goodwill in all directions. You can do that, or count your blessings, or just have a sense of excitement for the possibilities that lie ahead. Either way, make sure to start your day as a creator of your experience, and then search for evidence of that creation in the moments that follow: the delight you take in the wind through the trees, the dignity you find in caring for your body, the willingness you have to work with whatever comes your way.

96. ∾ BEAUTY STANDARDS

The idea that we ought to be past all our troubles by now, the idea that our hearts should fit the shape of some philosophical truth— these ideas are as damaging as the idea that our bodies should fit the shapes we find in magazines. You might think the most beautiful thing in life is excellence, you might think your task is to drag your bleeding fingers more nimbly across the violin of your days, but there is something more beautiful than precision: the relief that comes from letting all things be what they are. What is true is beautiful. Our need to attain some standard of success with our lives blinds us to the fact that the most beautiful attainment is just to have fewer needs. So today, remind yourself: "Everything true is beautiful." If it turns out to be true that you end up alone, you will find beauty in that. If it turns out to be true that you experience failure, you will find beauty in that. A moment of compassion for your life as it is is worth more than all the hours you spend preparing in the mirror.

97. ∽ DIFFERENT SPEEDS

Spiritual practice is not just a matter of slowing down. It's not all mindful chewing and long walks in the forest. The point of practice is to see what you are doing with your mind, and to learn how to better use it to live a more joyful life. To do that, learn to think and act at a few different speeds. Sometimes you need to settle down with just one thought or activity. Other times you need to speed up your thinking, just as a pilot might engage the throttle to safely get through a rough patch. The basic principle is this: when your mind is on things that are bringing you happiness, keep it there, unhurried, as long as you can. When you are being beaten and blown around by your fears or sorrows, get the hell out. Scramble through your blessings and good thoughts until you find one you can connect with. If you've developed a sense of ease in your breath, focus on that, but often, when the mind is dark, the breath can feel like a prison. So think on your feet and don't lose sight of the goal. We aren't here to win prizes for either speed or slowness, but to do what needs to be done in order to be happy.

98. ∽ BEYOND RECIPROCITY

In love, the greatest task is this: to care more about how you feel about the other person than you care about how the other person feels about you. This asymmetry scares us, for we have been taught to think that feeling loved depends upon finding perfectly reciprocal relationships, and we become terrified when we see cracks in that reciprocity. But in fact, your ability to feel loved starts with your ability to focus on the goodness in life and in those around you, and it is only around a strong focus of this kind that a strong relationship can ever grow. So your work is not to trap the right mate or become a more worthy person, but to develop your attention, every day, with everyone you meet, so that you can see the best in any situation. When you find yourself doubting that you are lovable enough or strong enough or sexy enough or whatever enough for someone else, learn to flip the perspective and ask instead: "What do I actually like about the other person?" Sometimes, the truthful answer is "nothing," in which case it's time to move on. But usually the problem is one of awareness rather than circumstance. So give yourself permission to take time to find the brightness in others and let that brightness flood your mind and heart. In true, loving appreciation, there is no pain or humiliation, and the only thing you need to give up is your habit of prioritizing a million things other than the delight you take in the person standing right before you.

99. ∾ THE LAMP AND THE MIRROR
Appreciation is not a scarce commodity. If you want to feel more appreciated by others, learn to better appreciate others. For the light belongs equally to the lamp and the mirror that reflects it.

100. ∾ PATHS IN OTHER PEOPLE'S EYES
We need relationships. We need to be alone too, but the danger in being alone is that, in solitude, our blind spots more easily remain invisible. Left alone with a single, unimpeachable version of ourselves, we don't experience the parts of our minds we have exiled or integrate them back into our lives. Without relationships, our growth is stunted. If we clearly saw the mirror that every human connection—no matter how difficult—is, we would be more grateful for others and less anxious about the agreements and negotiations we so often confuse with love. The first step to having a healthy relationship is not meeting the perfect person or settling on a vision of the future, but beginning where you are and paying attention to what has your attention right now. Do you find yourself fuming about a family member or co-worker? That relationship probably

has hold over all the others. So today, pay particular attention to the interactions that make you want to run, and remind yourself what a tremendous benefit they are to you. Even when people mistreat you, they are showing you what is left to learn: better setting of boundaries, perhaps, or how to strengthen your focus on what is good in the midst of all that isn't. Give thanks for others, difficult though they may be, for there is no roadmap to your life, just the paths of trial and error that you find in other people's eyes.

101. ～ SEEING AGAIN

When we feel unseen by others, we tend to withhold our seeing from them. What follows is a plague of invisibility that descends upon all our lives. It is the practice of generosity that restores our sight. When we give from the heart, no matter how others respond, we begin, once again, to perceive our own innate goodness. So today, try to show up for someone else in some way, and notice how, in doing so, you yourself come into focus like shapes held up to the light. For generosity indeed is like the sun, and provides us not only with warmth and comfort, but with vision too.

102. ～ THE VASTNESS OF OTHERS

Being able to see the good in others is a form of abundance. Our culture tends to talk about abundance in terms of getting stuff, but the truer meaning of abundance is having a mind that is spacious enough to perceive the good and bad in everything and choose between them. I once was in the company of a monk when the subject of Chögyam Trungpa, a controversial meditation teacher, came up. I was a little uncomfortable because I was sure the monk would have unfavorable things to say about Chögyam Trungpa's famous excesses. Instead, the monk told a beautiful story about how Chögyam Trungpa had once taken great pains to restore a statue of the Buddha. His choice of story taught me about what a person is, about how vast and varied we all are, and about how important it is to keep that vastness in mind when dealing with others. So today, when someone does something you don't like, you don't have to pretend you agree. Instead, try to place that person's actions within a larger space of awareness. Remind yourself that you are trying to understand all of life, not just one little part of it, and see if you then you can't find something good to think about the other person. As my teacher says: "You're going to be thinking all day long, so you may as well find something good to think about."

103. ~ WANTING OTHERS TO BE FLAWED

Practice picturing others succeeding without your help. One of the subtle parasites that eats away at relationships is the secret desire for others to be flawed so that we might forgive or fix them and thereby secure a place in their hearts. But when you focus on the weaknesses of others in order to strengthen your own position, not only do you do them no good, you also end up pushing them away. Others instinctively feel that your love is at odds with their growth and will chafe against the bit of your affections. So today, when someone lets you down, instead of getting angry or self-righteously forgiving, simply picture this person finding the true causes of his or her happiness. You may find this visualization hard at first, but remember that when you see people as hopeless you do not see them at all, so keep making an effort to see things another way. Picturing things differently is the first step to feeling things differently, and feeling things differently is the first step to changing your life.

104. ~ FAITH IN OTHER PEOPLE

If you want to develop confidence in yourself, don't gossip. We know that gossip isn't good, but we often think there's no harm in it as long as the other person doesn't find out. But the real problem with gossip is that it is a petri dish in which your own self-doubts can proliferate freely. For whatever the details are, all gossip basically says the same thing: "Look, that person wasn't able to succeed." And the reason we delight in that message, of course, is that it lets us off the hook about our own lack of success. When we gossip, what we're saying is, "Other people are my excuse for believing that I don't have what it takes to accomplish my dreams." This is how doubt gathers momentum. So when people around you are gossiping, one solution is to be silent. Another is to steer the conversation into an understanding that everyone's happiness depends on his or her own actions, which means that all people are still in process of finding their way. In the end, your faith in other people is really just faith in yourself.

105. ⁓ WILDFIRE CROSSING A MEADOW

If you want to live with more wisdom, pay attention to the wise beings all around you. There are times when we look at the world and see nothing but flawed individuals. But this is a misunderstanding of what wisdom is and how it travels, for just as a wildfire does not cross a meadow in one leap, but rather, by jumping from blade of grass to blade of grass, so too, wisdom does not travel through perfect individuals, but rather, through the good qualities of imperfect ones. So give yourself time today to take inventory. How many beings, past and present, have shown you kindness? How many have shown you generosity? Truthfulness? Patience? The value of hard work? What else could wisdom be other than these good qualities, which remind us of our own goodness and the joy inherent in being alive? As you search for these qualities in others, begin to take on these qualities yourself. That way you become a torch bearing wisdom from everyone you have ever met. So make it a practice today to seek out wisdom, not in what is written on a tea bag or in some ancient book, but in how you choose to see the others with whom you share this life.

106. THE VULNERABLE TRUTH

There is no teaching, and no truth, without vulnerability. Look at the Internet: a world full of voices all trying to educate each other, yet failing miserably, not because of a lack of knowledge, but because of a lack of softness. Like that Aesop's fable in which the North Wind tries to rip the coat off of a traveler who only clings to his garment more tightly, our attempts to force others to recognize our points of view will fail so long as we do not reveal what is fragile and tender in ourselves. So today, make vulnerability a practice. Even in conversations with strangers, ask yourself: "What am I willing to risk showing in order to be seen?" It doesn't have to be some deep, dark secret. If you can simply state your needs and feelings without blaming others for them, you will have given the world something rare and precious. And when others do not hear you, learn to see this closing not as evidence that someone is wrong, but rather that sufficient intimacy has not yet been established. Worry less about defending the truth and more about becoming truthful. If you can do that, you will find common ground with everyone you meet.

107. ❧ OTHER PEOPLE'S EYEGLASSES

Know that self-reliance doesn't come from big ideals but from small moments of honesty. Trust in yourself. Every day is filled with so many little lies, each one forming a screen in the mind that impedes the light of awareness. This is how we come to lose our vision and put on other people's lenses, most of which are the wrong prescription. So hold tightly to your truthfulness today, moment after moment. It will show you what no one else can: how to push forward in

your life, how to tend to your troubles wisely, and how to breathe
through each fluctuation of confidence with love and acceptance.

108. ∾ You Don't Have to Steal Fire

We live in a beautiful world, but our eyes cannot be truly open to it
until we see that beauty is not a property of the world but a property
of the heart. Unless we realize that the sweetness we are seeking
is not an object but a way of seeing, our appreciation will always
turn to jealousy or greed. A good practice, whenever you encounter
something beautiful, is to look for the love and attention that went
into making it. If you see a pleasing piece of jewelry, think about
the skill of the worker who made it; if you see a beautiful sunset,
think about your own goodness mirrored in the goodness of nature.
But be vigilant, for all around you, there are people who will tell
you that beauty is a scarce commodity, that you have to fight or
compete or degrade yourself in order to stand in its warmth for
a moment. So remember that she who knows how to build a fire
doesn't have to steal it from another woman's house. Right now, for
example, you can look around and ask, "What is beautiful about
this moment?" If you worry less about finding a perfect example
of attractiveness and more about seeing to it that one moment of
grace—the rustling of leaves or the smile of a stranger—connects
to another moment of grace, you will find it easier and easier to
experience beauty everywhere. You will find it is enough just to be
alive, to be breathing, in this exquisite world.

109. ∾ Experience Teaches Nothing

It isn't true that experience teaches us anything. What experience
does is strengthen some parts of the mind and not others. As we
go through life, the strong parts of ourselves work harder and take
more responsibility for the whole, like the overburdened manager

of a store whose staff mainly consists of incompetent workers who just hang around, or worse, do damage when no one is looking. This is why most people, as they age, become more capable, but also more stressed: they are working with stronger, yet fewer, sides of themselves, and are wasting energy trying to keep power away from the untrained members of their inner staffs. If you want to find true peace in this life, you have to do more than just work hard with the parts of you that are already wise. You also have to deal honestly with the unresolved difficulties of your heart, to train these, and to find their hidden goodness and potential. Beware of those who tell you that this technique or that experience will rid you of anger, envy, or resentment. No servant of the heart can ever be fired, and yet all things in the heart can be made good with love and time.

110. ∾ THE THRILL OF ASKING QUESTIONS

Learn to ask "why?" of every action you take. Don't ask as adults do, out of impatience with finding permanent solutions and eternal truths. Ask as children do: for the sheer thrill of making connections, for the pleasure of seeing how every question causes life to bring together people, ideas, and experiences. Children don't ask why the sky is blue in order to get a head start on their science careers, but because they understand, implicitly, that asking questions sets in motion a process of unfolding that feels good, in and of itself. This thrill is available to you, no matter how long you've been alive on this earth. If you hate your job, for example, ask yourself why, not with the purpose of finding a new one more quickly, but because it feels good to focus on how you want to feel once this job is behind you. And if you feel bad about yourself, ask why, not in order to drink the poison of your flaws a second time, but because it feels good to focus on how you will feel once these difficult emotions are behind you. In a sense, the answer to every "why?" is, "because you want to be happy." But the question only matters if you let life answer it, and that is why your work is not to get to the bottom of all your struggles, but to put your mind on the little things that make you feel alive and trust that there is where your deeper answers are too.

III. ❧ A FEEL FOR WORDS

Learn to get a feel for words. It isn't important that you be a poet or a philosopher, only that you develop a felt sense of how language connects you to your wish to be happy. We often see words as an obstacle to feeling and try to bypass them, but the truth is that we think in words all day long, and until we get some control over this process of inner verbalization, language will always rule us, not the other way around. This mastery doesn't come from books; in fact, a lot of what we've come to value as "thinking" is a just enslavement to other people's ideas. Mastery over language comes from being able to test the effect that words have on your heart and on your body. Bring your awareness to the center of your chest and ask yourself, "What do I most need to hear right now?" Listen for what comes, and test each answer to see if it brings a sense of warmth, safety, or joy to your heart. You may find that many interesting ideas produce no felt effect, and other, simpler ones connect you to a surprising sense of purpose and aliveness. Some words resonate at certain times but not at others, so be careful about arguing with yourself over what is "true" in some eternal sense. Truth is not something you look up in an encyclopedia, it is what you discover within your fathom-long body. So begin with the truth of what you feel right now, and follow that with the best words you know. Do this as a dancer follows her partner, mirroring, but also changing, at every turn.

112. ∞ Wood Smoke

Learn to judge words not only by whether they persuade you, but according to the level of noise they introduce into your mind. For a thing can be true and still cause great confusion, like a strong piece of wood that burns only smoke.

113. ∞ Choosing Silence

Look after the silences you find in the course of this day. You might believe your life is nothing but an unbroken chain of commotion; you might believe you'll find no peace till you leave this city, but there is silence in everything as surely as there is space in every atom: silence between each of your footsteps, between each of your breaths, between each of your thoughts. What keeps you from perceiving the silence that is everywhere is your fear of intimacy with yourself,—your fear that, in the naked stillness, you might prove unworthy of the love you are seeking. And so you choose noise over silence, as a man might choose a new lover over an old one so he doesn't have to see himself reflected in another's eyes. So today, when the racket around you becomes overwhelming, remind yourself that you have chosen this commotion. Remind yourself that you only have a little time to find intimacy with the life you're living. And then listen deep within the roar of the wind and crowd and city, and see if you can't notice something blooming there: the seeds of your attention sprouting flowers of peace.

114. ∞ Paying by the Word

Talk isn't cheap. It only seems that way when we value things according to their immediate cost rather than their long-term ability to shape our lives. In fact, all that we are begins with how we speak to ourselves and others. Knowing this, we should live as though we have to pay for every word we use, for in fact, we will.

115. ❧ Give Thanks for Harsh Words Left Unsaid

Give thanks for harsh words left unsaid. There may be issues you still need to discuss, feelings you need to express, but if you have any doubts about the consequences of your words, chances are it isn't time to speak them. Before you can truly communicate from your heart, you have to see that the pressure you feel to erupt isn't coming from anything around you, but from unexamined conflicts within you: the parts of yourself you still can't accept. Anger, jealousy, and resentment are like teenagers that we, the supposedly mature parents, want to throw out of the house when they cause trouble. That's why we explode: we want to put outside what is disagreeable within us. But when you realize how much damage these younger parts can do beyond the walls of your mind, you will be more likely to hold them closer, to hold your tongue, and to hold space for the difficult conversations that must first take place in the silence within you. So today, when you find yourself struggling to keep back unkind words, instead of just gritting your teeth, try to cultivate gratitude for what has not yet been said and for all the times in the past when you didn't say what you would have later regretted—and notice if just by giving thanks in this way, some of what you thought was inevitable pressure in fact diminishes.

116. ❧ A Gatekeeper of Words

How long will you go on fighting over words? Even among the polite, it doesn't take much—a single syllable like "God" or "love" or "sin" or "shame"—for the mind to struggle and rebel against experience. Words are important: they can heal, they can comfort, they can guide. But it is also in the nature of words to be unpredictable, to mean more or less than anyone could foresee, to turn on their handlers like snakes grasped by their tails. At some point, you have to realize that perfectly agreeable words, like perfectly agreeable physical conditions, do not exist. So the next time someone says something that rubs you the wrong way, try to shift your focus from the question, "Do I agree with this?" to the question, "What can I learn from this?" Think of yourself less as a participant in a debate and more as a gatekeeper. You can decide who and what to let in. For in every utterance, there is some wisdom and some sustenance, and if all you gather from the remarks of obnoxious people is that they, like you, want to be happy (though their actions are misguided), that understanding alone will be of great benefit to you. So today, when others are speaking, put your attention on your heart and start to trust that, from this inner place of safety, love, and wisdom, the good that needs to come in will come in, and the harm needs to stay out will stay out.

117. ❧ DON'T SAY SORRY WHEN WHAT YOU MEAN IS THANK YOU

Don't say sorry when what you mean is thank you. There is value in making amends, but apologies find their truest meaning only in the context of gratitude: gratitude for the goodness of this life and for the people who have shown you that goodness. We all want to find forgiveness for ourselves and others, but what will we do with forgiveness once we have found it? We don't normally think that far ahead. We want rituals of discipline and punishment that will make things right, but we often lack any sense of what a good life looks like once these rituals are over. And so we go from one penance to another, from prisons of iron to prisons of spirit, hoping the word "sorry" will lead us somewhere good. But what is the end of all this atonement, if not to learn how to appreciate the life we already have? So the next time you hurt someone, apologize yes, but try to understand the great benefit that this person is to you, and thank him or her in words or silent intention. And the next time someone hurts you, before you rush to forgive, try to appreciate the growth that this conflict is bringing you. Your existence is not a debt to be repaid, but a precious chance to make the most of this short while we have together.

118. ～ THOUGHTS SEEP INTO YOUR BONES

Learn how to protect your intentions as you go through this day. Ajaan Lee used the image of a healing cream. For the cream to work, you have to do more than just put it on: you have to leave it on, and make sure nothing rubs or washes it off. The same is true of our intentions, which often fail to have their desired effect not because they lack power, but because we lack consistency. For example, you might have the intention to meet this day with love and hope and joyful energy, but if a moment later you start thinking about this worry or that resentment, your original intention never has time to get under your skin. So today, try to protect your intentions with what is most constant in your experience: your breath. Notice what your attitude to life is right now, and if that attitude isn't serving you, change it. And then bring your mind to your breath, make the breath comfortable, and try to feel the effect that comfortable breathing has on your body. Have the perception that your breath, like your intentions, is seeping into your body, being absorbed by your bones. Don't try to force anything; just let the work do its work. Forget about all your well-worded goals and just soak in the breath right here. A few minutes of easeful breathing will bring you more guidance than all the coaches, calendars, and books in this world.

119. ～ Strange Days Indeed

Pay attention to the anomalies you find in this day: the unexpected building you pass on your commute, the old friend who contacts you from out of the blue, the piece of text on a bus that calls to your eye. At first, just practice noticing these things, delighting in what catches your eye like a child choosing a crayon. But then gradually start to see these details as signs of how you want to feel. Ask yourself: "What is there in that building, old friend, or bus ad that is calling me to expect more of my life?" You don't have to believe in superstition or cosmic conspiracy; you just have to believe in the intentional structure of your mind, which only notices things it has already invested with meaning and desire. What you are looking for in every moment and every detail, whether you are aware of it or not, is the sensation of being at the heart of your life's unfolding, like a surfer perfectly balanced on the crest of a wave. And though sometimes you may find yourself lost in frustration (too far ahead of the wave) or self-doubt (too far behind it), whatever disrupts your routine has the capacity to remind you that you are, in fact, exactly where you need to be. So cultivate gratitude for the strangeness in every day. Let it teach you the balance between doing and receiving.

120. ∾ LEARN HOW TO TAKE A GIFT
Learn how to take what is freely given. For though generosity is the first and greatest skill we must learn in order to be happy, skillful giving also depends on skillful taking. All beings subsist on food, mental and physical, and if you don't learn to feed where feeding is harmless, you will end up hungry, resentful, and bound to cause harm to others. So today, look around at all that life is offering, and ask yourself: "What is being freely given to me right now?" Learn how to take an opportunity when one presents itself. Learn how to take a gift. Learn how to take a compliment. And then go further, beyond the outer world and into your own mind, the greatest source of sustenance there is. Learn how to take joy in your inner blessings: the life in your limbs and the fierce determination in your heart. And then breathe, and let yourself feed on the breath, taking

from it whatever you need: peace, energy, imagination, consolation. Picture your body covered with millions of tiny holes, and imagine the breath coming in easily through all these points at once, filling you as full as you have ever been. Stop trying to purge yourself of this or that. We are neither here to starve nor to steal, but to learn how to grow our own food and sit down at the table to enjoy it.

121. ∾ TWO FEET
Desire and contentment are not opposites. They are the two feet on which a life moves forward.

122. ∾ THE LOOSE GARMENT OF DESIRE
Desire heals or wounds according to how we prepare for it. Our culture teaches us to think of desire as a sudden fall, like jumping out of a plane with no parachute. Our advertising tells us we have no choice but to jump; our religion tells us the best we can do is hope some higher power will catch us. While desire can feel sudden, it is actually a living, growing thing that we have been cultivating for a very long time. As such, we can learn to work with desire, to understand it, and to make the most of it. Desire is like a rhubarb plant, whose leaves are poisonous but whose roots are nourishing. Its medicine, at heart, is to remind us that our lives are supposed to feel good. Our problem, though, is that we keep eating the leaves— those particular experiences and pleasures we fixate on—and keep getting sick. So just as an herbalist must learn the different parts of a plant, we must learn the different parts of desire. Whatever there is in desire that causes you to remember that you are a creator of your experience, not just a consumer, is healthy; whatever causes you to forget this truth is not. The practice of appreciation will help you see this difference. If you can make it a habit to count your blessings every day, not only will you feel more blessed, but you

will also learn to hold desire with a gentler touch. You will see that there are countless points of attraction that can remind you of the goodness inside you, and in seeing this, you will come to wear desire not as a hairshirt, but as it is said in Christian tradition, as a loose garment that grazes your skin but doesn't constrain you.

123. ∽ Which Way Is Up?
Be careful about measuring your progress according to your current mood. You might be at the lowest point of the highest mountain. You might be at the highest point of the lowest valley. You cannot see the whole landscape of your life, nor do you need to. All you have to know, at any moment, is which way is up.

124. ∽ Coziness
Our ability to feel safe and protected in this life depends in large part on our level of gratitude. In Danish, I am told, the word *hygge* means both "coziness" and "thankfulness," a reminder that all true shelter originates in the heart. Too often, we direct appreciation only to external things, and so our gratitude becomes like a sweater full of holes: it only keeps us warms when the winds of circumstance blow in the right direction. But if we want to develop a seamless sense of warmth, one we can carry into all situations, our gratitude must encompass our inner qualities too: gratitude for our innate kindness, generosity, and ease of being apart from anything in the realm of the senses. So take joy in the blessings within you and don't worry that you are being immodest. (They are not *your* blessings, after all; they are yours to appreciate, not possess.) Try to make your gratitude as continuous as you can. For good fortune is never reliable, but in gratitude we find ourselves fortunate just the same.

125. ∽ Gratitude for Actions

Let your gratitude be for actions, not just for things. In the end, our actions are our true possessions. Enjoy the meal before you and the warmth around you, but know that these things are passing from our lives. We too are passing, but in the acts of kindness, care, and attention that we bring to ourselves and others, we carry each other into a timeless warmth, a deeper permanence we can cherish with our whole being, not just our minds. Be grateful, too, for your inner deeds: your ability to turn, time and again, to the heart and its priorities, and in so doing, shape your life. Truly you have built a home you can treasure. So let today be what it is: both everything and nothing. As a thing, it is just a day. And yet in it you will find a thousand chances to change your life.

126. ❧ DESIRE FOR WHAT YOU ALREADY HAVE

The truest expression of desire is desire for what you already have. You may think you want a lot of things that you lack—experiences, relationships, passion, recognition—and yet, behind and before all these desires, there is within you an inner sense that already knows the joy these outer things are supposed to bring. When you suffer over what you lack, that suffering, too, lies within you already: it is an ancient feeling you have chosen many times before. And so the "work" on yourself that remains to be done is not the work of willpower or painful exertion, but the work of awareness. In every moment, there is something you already have that you must learn to want more and more, for whatever you focus on grows in your experience, and no matter how stunted the tree of your life may seem, its roots are firmly fixed in the present. You may not have found the partner you are looking for, but the qualities that person possesses are right here, in you and in the good people you know. Focus on those qualities. You may not have found the bliss you are looking for, but the seeds of wellbeing are scattered throughout your life and body. Focus on those seeds.

127. ∾ THE GENTLE NUDGING OF A RADIO DIAL

If your conscience tells you to make a little more effort, then make a little more effort. But if your conscience tells you to make a lot more effort, ask yourself if you truly understand what effort is. For the extra effort needed to live and love well is usually the softest imaginable, like the slightest turn of a steering wheel or the gentlest nudge of a radio dial. Most movements greater than these only put the soul off course and out of tune. So ask yourself: "What small thing could I do today that I could do joyfully, over and over, for the rest of my days?" In the answer to this question lies the seed of greatest growth.

128. ∾ THE ONLY WINDOW

We often use discipline to compensate for lack of focus. We get up early and go stand by the window, but then we forget to look through the window. Why? Because focus, unlike discipline, opens us to the uncertainty of the present moment. It is in the window of that moment that you can see how fast life is passing. And yet it is only in that window that you can see life at all.

129. ∾ NON-REQUIRED READING

You don't need so much structure. You need a little structure, but more importantly, you need to learn to use structure wisely. There is in all of us a fear of no longer being a student, a fear of graduating to the point where we trust ourselves fully. And so we cling, not just to institutions and routines, but also to the vague-but-persistent doubt that we could never know what we are truly feeling. We prefer to think of ourselves as repressed or inexperienced rather than to take on the responsibility of guiding ourselves through life. Of course, there is always more to learn from others, but we must be careful to put that learning in the service of living, not the other way round. So before we pick up any practice or idea, we must be clear that no thought that doesn't serve our happiness is ever required. In the confusing years just after I received my doctorate, I didn't go to bookstores for a while, because I would always leave them feeling anxious about how much I hadn't read. Now I love bookstores, but only because I tell myself, before entering them, "None of this is required." The proper expression is "food for thought," not "obligation to think," so make sure your food is nourishing, and make sure to eat only when you are really hungry.

130. ∿ BALL OF DOUGH

As you go through this day, try to listen to your inner voice. We often think the phrase "inner voice" is a metaphor for something else—some philosophical truth, perhaps—but if you draw your awareness within, you will start to hear the words you are saying to yourself, moment by moment, as clearly and audibly as though they were spoken out loud by another. This is your command center, the place from which, knowingly or unknowingly, you are shaping your life. At first, as you practice what T. S. Eliot called "auditory inwardness," you may hear a confusion of voices, like the sound of children yelling in a cafeteria, but as you listen intently, you will find one voice rising to the fore: a kind, yet firm voice, much like the voice of a parent you may never have had. And as you focus on that voice and allow yourself to become one with it, you will find it has the power to gather together all your scattered, confused thoughts into one intentional thought, like a ball of dough picking up stray bits of flour. In doing this you will find you have the power to accomplish great things, or maybe just take care of yourself, the greatest accomplishment of all. So today, notice when your thoughts are thinking you rather than the other way around, and search for the voice that is great within you. What starts as a whisper from the galleys will one day become the captain of your soul.

131. ∾ ONE HUNDRED AND NINE AMUSEMENT PARKS

True discipline is the ability to remember what is joyful in whatever you are doing. Our culture has separated discipline from survival and pleasure and turned it into an abstract concern with "counting reps"—not just at the gym, but also at work, in our creative lives, and in our spiritual practices. I once met a man who told me that Florida is the most fun state because it has 109 amusement parks, and when I objected that I don't enjoy even one amusement park, he replied, "Yes, but 109! That's amazing!" That's pretty much our approach to discipline. We think we have to make the numbers in order to take joy in what we do, not realizing that it is joy that gives us the focus necessary to accomplish great things. So today, watch that your tools of productivity do not become new ways to kill joy. Pick one thing you want to do but can't seem to get around to, and make it your goal not to be productive in that area, but rather, to remember all the things you love about that activity. If you are trying to write a novel, write about what you love about writing. If you are trying to meditate, reflect on what you love about meditation. As you exercise your appreciation rather than your sense of struggle, you will find that your body and mind match your level of joy with energy, and you can get rid of the word "discipline" altogether.

132. ∾ SWEETNESS FROM DIFFERENT ANGLES

The opposite of laziness isn't discipline, but imagination, for laziness and discipline are just two names for the same misdirection of energy from what you love. But if you can let one thing capture your attention a thousand ways, you will find the strength to work on it a thousand days. So do not clamp down on what you love, but hover close to it as a bee hovers around a flower: tasting its sweetness from different angles, but also feeling its presence even when there is no contact.

133. ∾ DEBT COLLECTORS

Willpower is like a credit card: with it, you can change your life very quickly, but eventually you will have to pay back what you have borrowed from your body, your mind, and your heart. This is the problem with so many New Year's resolutions, which satisfy one part of the mind only by placing a burden on another. Eventually, the parts that have been pushed around want back what they have lent, and the whole project of transformation unravels. The true currency of change is joy: it is by developing thoughts of gratitude for the process of your growth (however difficult it may be) that your whole mind gets involved and your gains come to be lasting. Gratitude can be cultivated out of nearly anything, provided you use some ingenuity. So wherever you are today, however stuck you feel, make sure to acknowledge the patience, persistence, and wisdom you are developing and cultivate gratitude for them. Don't wait till your goals are reached to start being grateful, for that is like waiting for your bills to be paid to start earning money. Attend to the brightness of your mind right away, and your heart will leap up to do the work that must be done.

134. ∾ SLOW-TURNING GEARS

Write down all the things you want to do today, then try to do half. And then, if you accomplish half of that half, take joy in your effort. For strange as it sometimes seems, it is much easier to think of everything than to actually do something. We tend to push forward in our minds like a person pedaling a bike with no chain. We need to recall the feeling and the miracle of turning the gears even just a fraction of an inch.

135. ∾ OUTBIDDING PROCRASTINATION

You cannot defeat procrastination just by struggling to work harder. Procrastination is not mainly an issue of laziness but of self-interest: when you procrastinate, your mind is giving itself a reward in order to compensate for some perceived stress or threat. So you have to understand what the stress is and "outbid" it by promising an even greater reward. That could be something material, such as taking yourself out for a nice dinner or a walk, but in the end, the greatest reward you can give yourself is a mind that can think construc-tively. Maybe your procrastination is coming from a sense that you are working for others, not for yourself. If so, translate what you have to do into a language of self-care. You can think, *I'm getting my boss this assignment so I can make money and take care of myself.* Maybe your procrastination is coming from a fear of failure. If so, remind yourself that you will certainly fail in many ways, and the sooner you get around to making mistakes, the sooner you can grow from them. Whatever the issue is, look beyond your to-do lists toward the adventure and the possibilities that come from learning to think more skillfully. For we are not here to chain the wild horses of our minds to a post, but rather, to learn how to ride them.

136. ∾ LIFE IS NOT A DATA CHIP

Our society tends to confuse organizational tools with creativity. And we extend this same confusion to the pursuit of happiness, by believing that our fulfillment lies in acquiring and processing as much experience as possible. But life is not a data chip, and no matter how much we try to fill it, we still always get exactly twenty-four hours of experience every day. What we are seeking lies elsewhere—not in experience, but outside it, in our ability to reflect on the flow of life, as the sun reflects on the river: with brightness, but without drowning in it.

137. ∾ THE COOK AND THE FIRE

I wish I'd been told when I was younger that creativity and joy are the same thing. Instead, I was taught that artists struggle while consumers enjoy themselves. But that isn't true: there is little joy in consumption and little art in struggle—not in the long run, at least. And so you must remember that the art of connecting to creativity and joy is the art of discerning, in every moment, the difference between what you must do and what you must allow. A cook selects ingredients, prepares them, and cares for them, but he doesn't cook them: the fire does that. Writers tend to their words, painters to their colors, meditators to their breathing, but in all these activities there is a fire that must be left to do its own work. That fire is creativity or joy—the name makes no difference—and even where there is hard work to be done, the fire of joy must be tended to. So today, remember that your work is not to accomplish but to prepare: to put yourself in position, if only for a few minutes, to appreciate your life and its fertility. You have enough time to do that. It only takes a moment to remember the flame and let it work on you through the course of the day.

138. ∾ DICTATION

If you want to live an inspired life, then think of inspiration not as the discovery of something new, but as the transcription of what you already know. Like those prophets in religious stories who took down the words of angels, you will find value and completion in your work only when you begin to understand it as passing along a gift you have been given. Don't torture yourself with the idea of originality. If you can embrace your place in the web of existence, you will always be original. Let your task be simple: rise, and deliver the message you were sent to carry.

139. ∾ BODIES IN MOTION REMAIN IN MOTION

Look for evidence of positive inertia in your life. We usually focus on negative inertia: the ways we are "stuck," and the ways we haven't gotten around to the things that really matter to us. But in focusing on negative inertia, we forget the other half of Newton's First Law: that bodies in motion remain in motion unless acted on by another force. In other words, every act of self-care you perform, no matter how small—taking a walk, calling a friend, counting your blessings—sets your life in motion in a positive direction, and you will remain in that direction unless you allow the forces of restlessness, fear, and self-doubt to slow you down. So just as a skateboarder learns to rest in the momentum of the wheels, so too you must learn to rest after making some effort to change your life. Become intimate with the feeling of "gliding" that every positive action creates. Your breath will teach you this best: as you focus on your breath and try to make it comfortable, you will see that every easeful breath creates an even more easeful breath, and so on and so on. So let the effort you make in this life be small yet sustained. It doesn't matter how far you think you have left to go. If you don't stop yourself, you will get there eventually.

140. ∾ MASTERY

Our culture doesn't value the concept of mastery much, probably because it confuses it with perfection, and of course no one is perfect. But mastery is the confidence that the discovery of what you don't want will somehow lead to the discovery of what you do want. Without this possibility of mastery, no accomplishment or happiness is possible in this life: every wrong note would wreck a composer's work, and every feeling of sadness would drive a person off a ledge. So when you feel stuck in your life, remember that you are developing mastery, not merely passing through a series of random, unfortunate circumstances.

141. ❧ REPETITIVE INTELLIGENCE

A path is made by walking the same ground. If intelligence is to be in the service of life, it must involve repetition—repetition of the same truths, the same practices—until we understand the greatest repetition of all: our human suffering. If you don't have the patience to repeat yourself, you'll never understand what it is you are doing. Today you will have many opportunities to face the repetitions of your life and learn from them: the unpleasant people who keep finding you, the unskillful situations you keep ending up in. Guard against the thought that you are through with them. For if you truly understood their meaning and their causes, it is they who would be through with you.

142. ❧ RIDING A BICYCLE

We get so easily discouraged by our own bad moods, as though an hour of not feeling well were like being lost in the woods. In reality, a bad mood is more like stopping your bicycle at a traffic light: it does take a bit of pushing to get things going again, but it's not as though you must learn how to ride again. Momentum comes from appreciation, from cultivating gratitude for the blessings in your life. The trouble is we often try to move into too high a gear too soon. We try to be grateful for the entirety of our lives (with which we might be disappointed at the moment) or our partners (with whom we might be fighting at the moment) or our talents (in which we might not yet fully believe). Forget about building some cathedral of gratitude. Go for a walk, and as you walk, note all the things you see, however small, that make you glad. And then try to move beyond these things themselves, to reflecting on the gift that it is that you have the ability to choose what you put your attention on. If you can do this, you will start to feel a sense of acceleration in your body and mind. Don't worry about how far along the path you've come. A path is made by walking, and for now, take joy in your body's forward movement through space.

143. ∾ THE CAPTAIN'S GOOD SIDE

Try to make friends with the present moment, for it is the captain of the ship on which you are traveling. If you come to it, as we often do, with only demands and agendas, it will not take you where you want to go. If the present moment seems tough or uncaring, remember that you have not yet earned its trust either. You must come to it with something in your hands: some appreciation, some willingness to listen. Keep reversing every experience by asking what you can give to it. If you think and live this way, you will find yourself in a world that is no longer random, a world in which cooperation exists in all things. After all, the journey you are making is everyone else's too.

144. ∾ FINDING THE TRAIL AGAIN

Give thanks for the wide road you are traveling on that is leading you to a better life. However far you think you have come, the road is still open to you, and unlike a physical trail, the trail of your happiness is always right here in the present moment, accessible as soon as you start to change your mind and appreciate your blessings. Try to distinguish between true fear and false fear. False fear laments that you've already missed the last train. True fear warns you that there are many trains to come, but only this life in which to travel. The sooner you understand this, the sooner you will get on the next train, and the sooner you will start to keep watch over your mind to make sure the thoughts you think are vehicles worthy of the destination you desire. So today, when any thought interrupts your gratitude, ask yourself, "If I keep thinking this way, what will I become?" The more you ask this question in earnest, the better you will see how life works. And this is the greatest blessing: that life can, in fact, work, that it is not a random collision of events but a set of raw materials from which we can build a path that leads to the life we were meant to live.

145. ∾ No Child Left Behind

If you want to have a sense of direction in your life, you have to resist the idea that certain parts of yourself are more important than others. We tend to see self-improvement as a struggle between our different sides—a productive side and a side that wants to sleep all day, for example. But we don't have sides, we have parts: parts that we must integrate, not choose between. And like children, your parts need to be listened to more than indulged. We try to satisfy all our desires because we are actually scared of listening to them. In reality, desires are just voices of concern; they are reminders of what still lies unfulfilled within us. They are not, for the most part, commands to act. A desire for food might not be real hunger, but a reminder that you aren't feeling enough comfort right now. A desire for another person might not be an actual need for sex, but a reminder that your heart isn't getting enough love or intimacy. As we listen to our desires instead of acting on them, we realize that, though they are varied, they are capable of forming a consensus, just as a nation that listens to its minority voices will find that these groups, too, may actually want to be part of the fold. So the next time you feel you aren't making enough progress in your life, ask yourself, "Whom am I leaving behind?" Find that part, and give it feet to walk with and arms to pull the train of your life forward.

146. ∾ DEEPER, NOT HIGHER

Try to see your life as a process of deepening, not a process of climbing. There may be many things you want to accomplish, but the key to success in all cases is the same: take stock of what is already working and push the limits of that as far as you can. You may want to find a partner, for example, and yet you have already found love in so many forms. Focus on these and watch as the loving elements of your life grow and connect to each other. You may want to develop yourself spiritually, and yet you already have a basic goodness by virtue of being born. Focus on that goodness and watch as your path unfolds. Plato was right that the truth is always a recognition of something we have always known; though we fear complacency if we don't constantly treat life as a huge height to climb, it is actually the elaborate scaffolding in our lives that causes us to become discouraged and settle. You don't need to read all the books before you start writing your own. You don't need to climb all the ranks just to find out there's nothing at the top. Start today, wherever you are, scanning the horizon of your life for what brings you joy. There is no substitute for learning to love the exact spot on which you are standing right now.

147. ∾ A RUNDOWN BUS STOP

The present moment isn't necessarily pleasant. It's not a luxury resort where your dreams come true as soon as you enter—that belief is a setup for unhappiness. The present moment is more like a rundown bus stop at the center of town: chaotic, but the station from which all journeys begin.

148. ∾ Being In the Body

It's hard to develop wisdom until you can see that your life is supposed to feel good. We talk a lot about the importance of "being in the body," and it's true: your body is where your deepest wisdom lies. But your body is not just a lump of muscles and nerves; it is not just something you access in dance class or on a tennis court or during sex. Your body is every part of your experience in which you are sensitive to stress and ease. When you speak words and feel the healing or harm your words create, your words are your body. When you think thoughts and feel the healing or harm your thoughts create, your thoughts are your body. So if you want to be "in" your body, you can't just do yoga for an hour and then let your mind and mouth run amok for the rest of the day. You have to keep asking, "Does this actually feel good? Is this creating pain?" and feel (wherever you can locate a felt sense) for the answer to those questions. As you begin to relate to your experience less in terms of "should" and "shouldn't" and more in terms of "ease" and "stress," you will make better decisions for yourself and those around you, and you will discover a deeper kind of health: the health of having arrived, and of being at home, in your fathom-long body.

149. ∾ A Habit Is a Living Thing

A habit is a living thing, like a plant. Your determination is the soil, your attention is the water, and your appreciation is the sun. And yet, there is something in the growth of a plant that is entirely beyond any human—a drive to live that no gardener can create but can only assist. The same is true of the good habits you are trying to cultivate right now: they require your care, but not your struggle. They have a will to thrive and will thrive if you don't keep pulling at their stalks to make them grow faster. This is true not only of physical habits, but also of mental ones, such as remembering to look for the best in people. In the beginning, it can be hard to put your mind on these wholesome thoughts, but you must remember that you are not fighting a dragon but tending a garden; healthy habits of mind, if given minimally good conditions, will take root in time. So today, try to make it a practice, not a discipline, to focus on your breath, your heart, and your blessings as often as you can. Let your practice have a sense of ease and positive expectation to it. For the training of the mind, as they say in Zen, is "no big deal": it is as natural as the sprouting of seeds, the falling of rain, and the heart's desire to follow what it loves.

150. ⮵ THE MASTER FLORIST

We think if we accomplish enough, a sense of self-worth will strike us like a bolt of lightning. But for the most part, the reverse is true: it is by first knowing what you are worth that you will find the strength and contentment necessary to do the things that will bring your self-worth into its fullest development. Like a master florist who perceives the quality of a flower in its seed, you must learn to see the fulfillment of your deepest desires already present, in some small way, right here in the life you are living. For no amount of success will ever make you feel successful, no amount of money will ever make you feel you have enough, and no amount of affection will ever make you feel loved—you must find these feelings within yourself today and water them with your appreciation. Whatever you are striving for, ask yourself, "How can I enjoy myself along the way?" and try to bask in the good feeling of just being on the road. Don't mistake this type of contentment for complacency, for complacency is a refusal to grow. Contentment is an acceptance of where you are in the process of growing. Just reach for the thoughts and experiences that feel good, and let the joy of these blessings suffuse your mind. For in the end, your joy is your greatest worth.

151. ∾ An Archer's Bow

It is nice to show gratitude, but much more important to be truly grateful. Most of us have a hard time acknowledging our blessings without immediately feeling anxious to pay back what we have been given. And while anxiety about giving back may lead to short bursts of kindness, in the long run, guilt about what you owe others will always turn into resentment about what they owe you. Don't let that happen. Remind yourself that if you owe anything, it is to take the temporary, limited gifts you have been given and turn them into something eternal and limitless: love, compassion, joy, wisdom. And to do that, you are going to have to own your blessings; you are going to have to take them into your heart and let them bring you joy, for it is only in the fire of your own worthiness that true gratitude can be forged. So if you want to bow to what has been given, then bow, but bow like an archer's bow that bends with strength and purpose. Draw the arrows of your blessings close to your heart, feel their power, and then let them fly out into the world.

152. ∾ Stick to the Plan

Learn to take joy in seeing things through to the end. We usually judge our actions on the basis of how they are received by others, and so we forget that no amount of praise, status, or material gain can ever bring a sense of completion to the work we do. Judged by these standards, our actions will never be enough. What brings a sense of completion to our work are the inner qualities we develop along the way—qualities of persistence, patience, and open-heart-edness—and while we may not perfect them in one life, the mere act of turning our attention to these inner virtues allows us to pause at the end of a long day, at the end of a long life, and rest content, knowing we did what had to be done with the time we were given. So today, notice your impulse to cancel plans, break promises, or throw what you have been doing in the trash. Ask yourself: "What good seeds would I be planting just by sticking to the plan?" Let yourself feel gratitude when you are true to your own word, for few treasures are as precious as consistency. We like to say that eighty percent of life is just showing up; if that's so, the remaining twenty is sticking around until the final curtain call.

153. ∾ VOWELS

Look after the vowels of your life, not just the consonants. For it is easy to learn the beginnings and ends of things, but far more necessary to live in the sound that unfolds between.

154. ∾ YOUR BREATH HAS ANSWERS

Your breath has answers to the problems you are facing right now. Years ago, after a silent retreat, a friend of mine said, "You know, for the longest time I thought that focusing on the breath was a metaphor for something else. But I see now that the breath is life at its most literal." Literally, beneath all your stories, all your bullshit, your breath is your real life, reflecting and sustaining who you are at your most essential, like those rivers that run beneath our great cities and nourish them from below. In your breath you see things in terms of stress and ease, not in terms of what someone told you you ought to feel, and it is from this purer vantage that you can see yourself as a being who is trying to come into equilibrium, a being for whom no problem is a problem when inner harmony is attained, a being for whom everything is a problem when this harmony is lost. So today, take a moment to articulate something that is bothering you, and then hand it over to your breath, just as you would hand technical matter over to an expert. Be with your breath as literally as you can. Follow each twist and turn closely, just as you would follow the movements of a dance partner. And then, when the dance is over, notice how the problem has changed, or whether there ever was one to begin with.

155. ∾ INK SPOTS

You are not here to figure your whole life out. Self-improvement is not something you owe anyone. It is not a debt, like those huge sums of money that rich countries trick poor ones into believing they have to pay. You are here simply for the good of it, to grow because it makes you happy to grow, to expand because you delight in that expansion. As such, your work is not to solve every problem in front of you or get to the bottom of every thought in your head, but simply to allow the joy you find in one part of your life to spread gradually into every other part, like an ink blot that slowly spreads across the page. You don't have to make yourself feel love for everyone at once, just wish people well as best as you can, avoid ill-will as best as you can, but understand, above all, that the opening of your heart in one direction is the opening of your heart in all directions. You don't have to manufacture any great passion for living. Just rest at ease, like a spider at the center of its web, watching for what comes across the horizon. Then seize that opportunity and cultivate something good: a bit of good humor, a bit of compassion, or maybe just a bit of patience. Do this not because you're supposed to, but because you can actually feel goodness in doing it. When you can feel appreciation for every situation, however big or small, you will see that unlocking one door opens up all the others.

156. ∾ DAMMING THE RIVER

Thinking is always a way of trying to control reality. No matter how much you flatter yourself that your mental chatter and conversations with others exist for the sake of knowledge or intellectual progress, the truth is that you think because you are frightened by life and are trying to gain some power over it. You are trying to dam a river whose endless succession of days and nights and changes, frankly, terrifies you. Of course, there can be benefit in damming a river, provided the dam is well built and well placed. In the same way, your thoughts can be beneficial if they are strategic and spaced between pauses that give them momentum and direction. So today, when you find yourself lost in thought, when your mind is like a dump truck randomly unloading boulders into the current of your life, remember the spaces between the dams. And you will find these spaces by learning to feel your thoughts rather than merely think them. Take a piece, a single sentence, from your inner monologue and ask yourself: "How does this feel in my body?" If it feels bad, stagnant, or untrue, try to find a thought that feels better. But remember the pauses, and remember to feel the ripples that each thought produces in you. For this is all you have ever wanted: not to pull the river, but to swim in it, and be free.

157. ∾ A Hunter of Good Thoughts

You can't expect that you will always wake up with a head full of happy thoughts. You have to learn how to hunt for good thoughts, just as any hunter hunts her prey. To do that, to become a hunter, you have to develop two contrasting skills: the ability to be very still and the ability to be very ready. There are plenty of passionate people who are ready to be happy, but who kick up so much dust with their passion that they lose the trail leading from the present moment to how they want to feel. And then there are people who don't have enough passion, who may be quiet and accepting, but who aren't paying enough attention to see the quarry that passes before their eyes. So wherever you are today, whatever mood you may be in, scan the horizon of your thoughts for one that feels right—maybe a joyful reminder of your blessings; maybe some tender compassion for your sorrows. Sit and wait for a thought that feels good to appear, and when it does, pursue it slowly, evenly, lest you scare it away with your hasty desire. The mind moves faster than any forest animal, but you have something better than speed: the ability to learn from every single thing that happens to you.

158. ∾ INTERRUPTING THOUGHT

We imagine our thoughts are the most human part of us, but they are often the most mechanical. The thinking mind is in many ways a machine that, left unchecked, runs according to program till it runs itself down. What is truly human is not our ability to think, but our ability to interrupt thought, to ask, "Do I need to think this way right now?" Our capacity for interrupting thought is a human freedom, but as with all freedoms, it is frightening, for we have learned from a young age that we are lovable depending on how we think; it can be hard for us to accept that we could be loved for who we are rather than what we do with our minds. So this is our great task: to be brave enough to switch off the machine and wait in the silence for a truer, more human version of ourselves to appear.

159. ∾ DON'T SEEK FAME

There is good reason not to seek fame. It is not that we were born to be mediocre, but rather, that we were born to be free. What we look to get from fame is nothing but freedom from resistance: freedom to love, work, and play without limitation. And yet, the desire for fame actually contains the opposite of all these: resentment, joyless exertion, and contraction of the spirit. In truth, nothing makes us more mediocre, and more unknown, than the desire to be known.

160. ∾ MONEY

The idea that you have to make money doing what you love destroys both creativity and spirituality. People often ask, "But don't I deserve to be supported for doing what I love?" and the answer is, yes: you deserve to be supported for your art, your passion, and every dream you hold in your heart. But the question remains, what will you do when you aren't supported? Will you bend the truth of who you are to fit the world, or will you understand that truth and the world are sometimes different? Wallace Stevens, one of the greatest poets of the twentieth century, was an insurance salesman who wrote poems on slips of paper while walking. You don't need so many hours to accomplish your dreams, and more money won't give you the sense of abundance you are seeking. We all need to feel exchange, but we narrow the possibilities of exchange by focusing on money, like some clichéd lover who can only feel love in the form of an expensive dinner or box of chocolates. If you want to be free, you are going to have to do some things for free, trusting that somehow you will be provided for. And the irony is: the less you fixate on money, the more opportunities for abundance you will find: new connections, new experiences, new kinds of sustenance for body and mind. So try to act with less fear. You deserve that, above all.

161. ∾ RESURRECTION

It is only by testing things that we discover we are free. This may be the truest meaning of resurrection: not that a privileged few among us are immortal, but that all of us, without exception, have the ability to elevate our minds above suffering, and even, ultimately, above death. We learn this not by looking for grace outside ourselves, but by examining the consequences of how we think about each moment. Instead of simply "having" feelings about life, we can learn to cultivate higher feelings, not in a dishonest way that ignores the walls still in our hearts, but with a mind to finding cracks in these walls—for there always are cracks. Right now, for example, can you reach for a thought that feels a little bit better than the one you were just thinking? Can you find a sense of comfort somewhere in your body or a sense of blessing in your recent memory? And can you hold your mind right there, aware that this ability to stay in one chosen place is itself freedom and the doorway to a kind of deathlessness? For it is not enough just to accept the world you see around you, a world you yourself have unknowingly created. You must now begin to know its creator.

162. ⌒ SUNLIGHT IN A SPANISH CHURCH

Never give up anything till you understand the benefit it has brought you. Good and evil are intertwined in every moment, and the light you are running toward is like the light in those Spanish churches that comes from gold once paid for with the blood of slaves. You may want to stand apart from the mess of your own history, but you cannot. And it is the same with every "toxic" habit or relationship you are now trying to put behind you: until you see that what you most want out of life has been shaped by your suffering, you will keep carrying that suffering along with you, no matter how much distance you put between yourself and your problematic habits or relationships. You will keep repeating history. So today, think of something you are trying to quit, and instead of focusing on how bad that thing is or how ashamed of yourself you are, try to understand the initial appeal that led you to it. Try to understand that all actions, healthy and unhealthy, come from your deep wish to be happy. And then try to find love for yourself in your heart, for it is only love that lets us separate freedom from addiction, only love that lets us start over again.

163. ∾ STEP INTO THE PUNCH

If you want to be less concerned with whether people like you, focus instead on what you like about them. Your ego will tell you that self-esteem comes from feeling indifferent to those who have rejected you, but in fact the opposite is true: the more you use indifference to defend yourself, the more indifferent the world around you will seem. If you can put your attention on other people's good qualities, you will find both an intimacy with them and freedom from their approval. You will also find those same good qualities arising again in other areas of your life, and in other people who can better love you the way you want to be loved. So when you feel the blow of rejection approaching, step into the punch, as a martial artist might, and remind yourself of what you admired about that person in the first place. Sometimes you will find there isn't much there, and the spell this person has cast on you will be broken. But more often, you will find a sense of gladness simply to have experienced this person and shared in his or her goodness. And for that moment, perhaps, you will know a love that is not weighed down by fear.

164. ∾ OLD-FASHIONED LETTERS

We move through life as though we are handwriting a letter we do not yet understand. Every mistake we make is permanent, yet every mistake leads to the discovery of something we never deeper that we always wanted to express but never knew existed in us. Those who live life as though before a blank computer screen, waiting for the blinking cursor to tell them something, will never understand the magic that happens when you stop trying to erase your experiences, and instead, try to continue on skillfully. Many accidents will come today: things you didn't mean to do or say, messes you will wish you hadn't made. Treat each of these as a sign of the fuller person you are becoming, and remember that what is difficult for you to express now will be a joy for someone else to receive later.

165. ✎ THE GARDEN OF FORKING PATHS

Gratitude is not optimism. It is not the blind hope that the universe is fundamentally good or that everything happens for some useful reason. To be truly grateful, you have to assume that life is basically chaotic, and that gratitude is a spontaneous choice about where and how to exist in that chaos. We inhabit a world like the one Borges described in his story, "The Garden of Forking Paths"; a world in which all possible outcomes occur simultaneously, each one leading to further possibilities, and so on. In the vastness of your life, you have already accomplished your dreams and been a total failure too. People adore you and are also disappointed in you. You are slowly dying and your best days are still ahead. In the labyrinth of every moment, many, many things are true, but where you exist within that maze depends entirely upon your level of gratitude. So today, when life shows you a dead end, remind yourself that you are only ever where your focus has taken you. All your mistakes, your flaws, your foolish repetitions may exist somewhere in the infinite space of who you are, but those things don't have to hurt you or anyone else right here in the present moment. Just put your mind on your blessings and your breath, and you will find you can change not only the future, but the past as well.

166. ✎ JUST BEFORE THE BOMB GOES OFF

Try not to confuse gratitude with feeling lucky. We are always saying things like, "Remember how fortunate you are," by which we mean, I suppose, that life is precious. But concepts of luck or fortune almost always carry with them feelings of guilt, on the one hand, or anxiety, on the other, two emotions that keep gratitude from ripening into joy. It takes a strong mind to remember that, though gratitude is a key to living well, you do not control the universe with it. Seeds planted long ago will still sprout in the future, no matter what you do. And in our constant comparisons of who has more or less suffering, who is more or less blessed, we forget that we are all the same in our impermanence. We all walking through the same airport just before the bomb goes off, recognizing the same joys and sorrows in the eyes of those we meet, taking in the beauty of this trembling, unmasterable moment. And what transforms us is not luck, but the ability to understand, just before it explodes, that this moment was always enough.

167. ∾ THE UNHURRIED HOURS

Try to leave open spaces in your days, for these unhurried, unstructured hours are a form of generosity to yourself, just like a college fund whose benefits show themselves more fully with the passing of years. Try your best to give this gift to yourself, but be careful about getting frustrated if your schedule won't bend to your will; in all generosity, there is a part you can control and a part fixed by circumstance. You only have so much money to give, for example, but if you can incline to non-material forms of giving, such as goodwill, compassion, or forgiveness, you will find your generosity limitless. It is the same with your time. You can only bring so much empty space to your schedule, but you can bring an unlimited sense of spaciousness to whatever you do. To do that, ask yourself, when you get pulled into some unwanted form of being busy, "What do I have to give right now?" If you can ask this question whole-heartedly, you will find that giving more gives you more to give. Time may not bend to your will, but it will bend to your heart.

168. ∾ The Architect

Don't waste your time regretting wasted time. Time that has passed is now part of the natural world. It is like trees and rivers, no longer good or bad, but part of the landscape you inhabit. The question is whether, like a skilled architect, you will find ingenuity to build a home where you stand. For some days open onto easy meadows and others collapse onto piles of stones. But there is always something to build upon, and a force within you that is restless.

169. ∾ Generous Attention

Attention is a form of generosity. Just as there is no connection between a person's wealth and how much she chooses to help others, there is no connection between the state of your mind and how much care you bring to each moment. In the midst of anxiety, darkness, and the feeling that your life is beyond your control, you still have loving awareness to bring to every experience. And you will give, as all philanthropists do, if you believe enough in the cause: yourself.

170. ∾ Hoarding Excitement

It takes courage to resist the pressure to be constantly excited by life. A lot of forced excitement is to happiness what hoarding is to prosperity: a feeling of scarcity dressed up as abundance.

171. ∾ Green Fruit in Bulk

If you want more clarity about your own life, learn to better appreciate the successes of others. Success is not something "out there" beyond you. It is a ripening of potentials that exist within us all, in different ways and at different paces; until you develop a taste for the sweetness of other people's ripening, you will not recognize your own when it comes. When you compete, compare, or try to beat someone else to a goal, you are like an anxious consumer who buys up green fruit in bulk, only to discover that what he has hoarded rots before it ever really ripens. The same is true of all your hard work and determination: the will never fully mature so long as jealousy and resentment obscure your heart. So today, when you start to feel cloudy or discouraged about your own life, open the scope of your awareness to include the victories of others, and count these as your own. Think to yourself, *May all beings not be deprived of the good fortune they have attained*, and try to feel the joy in that statement. For what does it matter if the fruit you eat was grown by this person or that one? If it is sweet today, feed on it, and know that the happiness it brings belongs to you too.

172. ∾ A Teacher of Life

Be a student of life always, but never forget that you are also a teacher of life. At every moment, you are actively teaching your experience, educating it, and training potentials within you that will ripen over time—all according to what you choose to focus on and how you choose to focus on it. We often confuse teaching with having power over others: we pay our dues, get certified, and then try to leave a mark on those around us. But as Bruce Lee said, "A good teacher protects his students from his own influence." This is true not just for their sake, but for the teacher's as well, for the more a person confuses education with control, the less he trusts in his ability to be happy regardless of the circumstances. For these reasons, a good teacher teaches only by power of example and makes sure his own house is in order. So today, instead of trying so hard to leave a mark on the world, turn to your thoughts, which are as much in need of your guidance as is anyone around you, and try to be a role model to these inner students. When anger, sadness, or anxiety arise, instead of trying to change or control them, focus on your blessings and your breath and show the rest of your mind that another way is possible. For what is most difficult within you is not simply disobedient, it is also what hungers for your leadership most. So lead from within, and tomorrow the world around you will be that much brighter.

173. ❧ MAY YOU NOT BE WEARY

Take some time to notice how hard everyone around you is trying. In Iran, it is customary to acknowledge when others are working by saying, *Khaste na bashi*—"May you not be weary." In America, we tend to respond to other people's labor by comparing their efforts to our own: "That person is lazy" or "Look at that sad sack slaving her life away." We don't realize that by comparing instead of appreciating, we cheapen the value of our own efforts by training ourselves to perceive the world as uncooperative and unrewarding. This is why most of us find work so disagreeable, for in ceasing to thank others, we come to find our own tasks thankless. So today, walk where people are working and silently acknowledge their efforts. And not just people scrubbing floors or lifting heavy things, but all the men and women taking care of themselves by running errands or just sitting together with those they love. Even when people's actions strike you as misguided, notice the struggle for happiness beneath what they are doing. Notice trees bending their branches toward the sun and bricks resisting the entropy of time. The whole world is flowering around you, and as you learn to see it with eyes of praise, you will see your own life flowering too.

174. ❧ NON-COMPLAINING

One definition of a good life is to be in a continuous state of non-complaining. Of course, the opposite of complaining isn't pretending that everything is fine. The real opposite of complaining is seeing that every moment is an opportunity to develop some aspect of your goodness. And to do that, you are going to have to find a skillful attitude towards what's coming up right now, not a one-size-fits-all smiley face. If you're getting really thrown by something, the skillful attitude is probably one of compassion for yourself, not joy. Often, it might be not one thing but many little crises that are plaguing you. In that case, the skillful attitude is probably one of equanimity: seeing that your happiness depends on your actions, not your chaotic circumstances. So today, when you find the world pressing in on you, remind yourself, "It isn't this situation but my relationship to it that will determine whether I'll be happy." Try to complain less with your mouth, but more importantly, use this practice of equanimity to complain less with your heart. For non-complaining is less about gagging yourself than it is about recognizing the advantageous position you occupy. So keep calm and remember: whatever mud you're stuck in right now is perfect soil to plant something good.

175. ∾ YOUR TRUE CAREER
Learn how to connect the small moments of joy in your life. Particularly in America, we depend so much on the idea of a career to bring us a unified sense of purpose and excitement about life. But a career (from the Latin word for "carriage") is supposed to carry you somewhere, and if you see it no further than money, status, or praise, then you are on a path that goes nowhere. Your true career lies in learning to make connections between the little things that open your heart: a sudden summer breeze, a song on the radio, the unexpected feeling of ease in some part of your body. If you pay attention not just to these moments, but also to the way they connect, the way they invite each other and flow together like drops of rain converging on a windshield, you will understand that joy is not a property of the world, but a property of your own awareness.

So try this today: start with an interval of two minutes, and see how many two-minute actions you can take in support of what makes you happy. Let yourself jump from action to action, as one might jump from stone to stone when crossing a river. Let your intuition carry you forward, and don't look back.

176. ◆ HEALTH IN DIVERSITY

Health is mostly a matter of diversity. We often think the problem is contamination, and so we close our bodies, our hearts, and our borders to whatever we find threatening. But there is very little threatening you from outside that is not already within you. Your physical being is literally teeming with lethal germs, and yet, as scientists have told us for years, a healthy body is not one that is free from bacteria, but one in which a balance exists between different microorganisms. Your mind works in exactly the same way. Happy people have the same dark, despairing, and frustrated thoughts as anyone else, but they have established a diversity of thinking that allows this darkness to coexist with the light. And the best way to accomplish this diversity is to practice gratitude, each and every day. Gratitude is not a practice of "being positive." That kind of antiseptic gratitude only brings more frailty. True gratitude is a practice of understanding how wide the range of the mind is, and how much joy there can be in the midst of difficulty. So today, try to develop some appreciation for the diversity of your mind. Try to understand the great benefit this inner variety has for your life. Open the borders of your heart just a little bit more. For you are stronger, far stronger, than you have led yourself to believe.

177. ◆ DEDICATE YOUR EATING

Since you are going to die, whatever you do and sooner than you realize, there is really only one good reason to take care of your body: to make it a vessel of love. I once saw an old man in a juice bar cursing out the staff for not preparing his juice correctly. He looked as absurd as someone struggling to rearrange deck chairs on a sinking ship. Yet even the more polite among us often forget what food is really for: we think we are eating to attain health or pleasure, not realizing how short-lived and insubstantial such attainments are. Of course, eating well can be an expression of love for yourself and others, but love is as love does. So the next time you sit down to a meal, instead of worrying so much about taste (for taste lasts only a moment) or even nutrition (for the body is fickle, no matter what you do), dedicate your eating to someone you love: another person, or maybe just yourself. You can think, *May this food bring happiness. May it make me strong enough to love.* For love does take some strength, and this is a side of the body-mind connection we rarely explore, lost as we are in trying to control physical experience. But a mind given a little sustenance and a lot of attention to joy and appreciation will always be at peace with the body as it is: fragile, inconstant, yet trembling with love.

178. ∾ LOST IN THE SUPERMARKET

We suffer greatly from the illusion that our preferences show us what truly makes us happy. Even spiritually-minded people will often say, "Oh, I like that teaching. I'm going to try that," or, "I don't like that teaching. I won't follow it." But if you look closely, the part of the mind that has preferences is like one of those price guns used in supermarkets: all day long it goes around labeling things as having this value or that value. Yet if you ask the price gun what all the food is for, or which kinds, or how much a person should eat, the price gun doesn't have any idea. You need a higher intelligence for that. So too, if you want to be happy, you need a higher intelligence than your preferences.

179. ☙ The Best That Can Be Expected

Learn how to raise your expectations. We often think that what we expect is determined by what we experience, but the fact that we can consciously lower our expectations shows that we can raise them too. In reality, there are no "higher" or "lower" expectations, there are only those that are better or worse for you at a given time. As with medicine, expectations heal or hurt depending on how they address the symptoms at hand. If you've been pushing yourself to be perfect at some job or relationship, the softer expectation that you will do well enough, or at least that you will learn something, may be the right one. But if you're feeling unfulfilled, it may be that you need to expect more—more clarity, more joy, more growth—from what you are doing. Play with different perceptions to see which one feels best. Before you begin any activity, meet any person, or enter any building, ask yourself, "What's the best that can be expected here?" and then reach for what feels both true and soothing. Remind yourself that you aren't trying to bend reality to your will, you are simply trying to enlarge the scope of what you believe is possible. For what we are really seeking in any situation is not just the presence of pleasure and the absence of pain, but the thrill of discovery, and though we may get lucky here and there, over the course of a lifetime we discover only as much as we intend to find.

180. ☙ Wisdom Knows Where to Dig

The raw materials of each day are different, and we will suffer if we cannot improvise. Who knows why a thought that made you happy yesterday brings pain today? Sometimes the weather of your mind has just shifted. Sometimes the fields of thought you have been sowing are over-harvested and need to rest. All that matters is that you serve things as they are, which means thinking according to how you want to live, not living according to how you want to think.

If thinking about your partner makes you upset right now, well then don't think about your partner. You don't need to orchestrate a confrontation or move out. You just need to draw from a different well. But there is water in so many places: in the little, lovely details that make this day different from all the others. So let your mind quench its thirst by recalling the blessings of this day, your own good deeds, and your life, with all its joys and struggles. And then give thanks for the wisdom within you that always knows where to dig.

181. ∾ COOPERATION
You will find as much cooperation in life as you look for. It's so easy to complain about the one knot in your back, even as trillions of cells in your body are cooperating to keep you alive. It's so easy to complain about the one person standing in your way, even as countless men, women, and generations have toiled, struggled, and organized to make your life possible. If you stop to think about it, the amount of cooperation you are experiencing at this very moment is staggering—but that's just it: you have to stop to think about it. And then you have to go further. You have to feel cooperation, not just know it intellectually. Feel how every breath you breathe is trying to bring equilibrium to your body. Feel how every word you speak is trying to bring harmony between your understanding and the truth of who you are. This world may be governed by chaos, life may lack an overarching design, and yet the forces of cooperation are right here before you. Seek them out, and let your awareness become one with them.

182. ∾ WRECKING PEACE
When we find a bit of peace, we often wreck it with the thought, *But how will this help me solve my problems?* We forget that the real problem is the mind's habit of dismissing what feels good and exalting what

feels difficult. No matter how small the ease you find today may be, don't be in a hurry to move on.

183. ∾ CURRENTS OF ADMIRATION

Surround yourself with people you admire, and then actually take some time to admire them. One of the reasons why life sometimes seems to go nowhere, why it appears as nothing but a long plateau with a sudden drop-off at the end, is that we have spent so much time finding flaws in others that our lowered expectations for them become lowered expectations for ourselves. Your ability to admire others, with both truthfulness and precision, is the same ability you need to find within yourself the starting point for your next phase of growth. So whenever you feel stuck or in a rut, ask yourself who in your life is pointing to the way out. Don't let yourself fall into jealousy, on the one hand, or cynicism, on the other. Your admiration creates a powerful current, like currents of air that can lift planes of steel, and you too will rise within it if you just let go of the rock to which you are clinging.

184. ∾ BECOMING ADMIRABLE TO YOURSELF

Try, above all, to become admirable to yourself. We often think that when trouble comes, our task is to get rid of it as quickly as possible, just as we often think that good parenting is a matter of protecting kids from conflict. But what kids need most is not to live in a perfect world, but to see their parents face difficulty with skill and love. And in the same way, your mind has child-like and vulnerable parts that need the power of your good example more than the absence of strife in order to feel safe and protected. You are watching yourself closely, so act accordingly. When friction arises, remind yourself that friction is part of this human experience and also an opportunity to develop self-respect. For when the mind becomes admirable to itself, it relaxes, and where there is peace, there is also the strength to let go.

185. ∾ OTHER PEOPLE'S LITTER

A lot of your worries are just other people's litter. They feel like yours because you pick them up, but now where will you put them? And how will you help the world with a head full of garbage?

186. ∾ MUSCLE MEMORY

One of the beautiful things about memory is that it can help us overcome our doubts about the future. Normally, we look back on the past only to focus on the pleasures we no longer have or to regret the stupid things we've done—and if we remember learning anything, we usually attribute this to luck or circumstance or the mere passing of time. This is how we keep repeating the past. But do you remember that time when your lover left you and you thought you'd die, but you didn't? And do you remember that time when you had no money and thought the world would end, but it didn't? What changed in you that allowed you to move from doubt into hope? If you recall carefully, at some point you released resistance to what was happening and just felt it, the way after a long cry you might find yourself feeling the sensation of your chest rising and falling. It is in these moments that we realize that most of our burdens are not overcome by carrying them to a finish line, but simply by putting them down. So try to build the sort of muscle memory that allows you to remember these moments of release, for that is how your faith in the future will be accomplished and your troubles met with a lighter heart. Like a gymnast who feels her way into a balance by remembering what that balance felt like before, you must feel your way into hope by looking back on your life and remembering that, somehow, suffering always comes to an end.

187. ∾ Practices Serve People

Peace and passion are the two feet on which a life moves forward. But like children learning to walk, we are usually leaning too far to one side, not yet able to feel the greater balance on which our progress depends. We often think, for example, that we have "good" or "bad" moods, rather than seeing these moods as indicators of what our next right step should be. This is one manifestation of our lack of balance. Often, people who deal with depression seem to seek out deep contemplative or meditative practices, when what they really need to do is go for a walk, call a friend, count their blessings, or find something to look forward to about the future. And just as often, people who deal with anxiety and stress seem to seek out busy, excited activities that involve a lot of planning and concepts, when what they really need to do is just focus on their breathing and let life work on itself for a while. We like to do what we're already good at, and this is where things get problematic. So today, try to ignore both your own preferences and the advice other people give you, and focus instead on developing what is underdeveloped. If your attempts at simplicity aren't giving you good results, make your life a little more complicated: go somewhere you've never been before; add one more thing to your schedule that makes you feel passionate. But if things feel too complicated right now, make a list of all the things you can happily procrastinate about, and then choose just one activity that brings you some peace. Practices are meant to serve people, not the other way around.

CONSOLATION

(autumn)

188. ∾ Real Transformation

Strive to become a better person, but never forget that a single moment of compassion for yourself is worth more than a million hours of self-improvement. If your body feels weak, you can go to the gym. If your mind feels dark, you can practice thinking pleasant thoughts. These are worthwhile pursuits, and yet, they are forms of conditioning, not forms of transformation. As soon as you stop putting effort into them, your mind and body will tend to revert to old habits of being. True compassion for yourself, on the other hand, will change you in ways that cannot be undone. So today, when your body hurts or your heart hurts, instead of rushing to fix the problem with this or that technique, make up your mind that you will just show up for yourself. Be there for yourself, as a parent would be there for a sick child: sitting by the edge of the bed, simply saying, "I'm not going anywhere. I will be here tonight and all the nights till you are well." Your body will break and your heart too may break, but as someone who has had his share of illness, I can tell you this: the secret beauty of sickness is finding out how deeply you are loved. And in this life, there is no surprise more wonderful than that.

189. ∾ There Is Always Something You Can Do

There is always something you can do. Whether you have committed a horrible act or have lived the life of a saint, whether you are suicidal or ecstatic, there is always a next right step. The point of any practice, worldly or spiritual, should be to remind you that you always have options, that no matter how many keys you have tried and failed with, there are still more on the chain of your human potential. But to understand your range of options, you have to go beyond the normal variety of physical actions and begin to explore the options of the heart. We believe we are supposed to feel one thing always, one unvarying type of satisfaction with our lives, and so we miss our complex emotions for the tools they are. Books and teachers can give you suggestions on how to live better, but in the end, you have to learn from your own feelings. So today, when a difficult emotion arises, ask yourself, "What use does this have?" Often, the usefulness of emotions has nothing to do with venting them, but rather with allowing them simply to be information. Anger, frustration, sadness, despair—these are some of the ways the mind alerts itself to what has been overlooked for far too long. So take joy in these inner tools, with which you will one day be able to measure and shape your life, and put some work into mastering them.

190. ∾ THE BURDEN OF POSITIVE THINKING
Lay down the burden of your positive thinking. It is better to focus on sorrow with love and compassion than to cultivate an idealism based on defensiveness or a desire to seem inspiring to others. The healing you are seeking is not found in words, but in the quality of intention you bring to all things. And to see this quality of intention, to see what you are really doing beneath the radar of language, you must make a shift. So stop trying to fix your troubles, and instead open your heart to them. Try less to perfect the map of your life, and more to find your true location within it.

191. ∾ HOLDING YOURSELF
You have to learn how to hold yourself. We all want to be held by someone else, but that isn't how we heal. True healing comes

from experiencing ourselves as duality: as one part that is vulnerable enough to feel pain, and another part that is strong enough to be there for the first. This duality isn't an idea. It's something you can begin to recognize in your awareness right now. So today, when pain comes—pain in your body or pain in your heart—locate the pain in your awareness and breathe all around it, holding it in breath as a mother might hold a child in her arms. Try not to fix the pain or force it to go away, for that will cause you to miss what is most painful about pain: the loneliness it triggers in us. Just stay right there, hovering around what hurts with tenderness and patience, and it won't be long before you know what it means that you are never alone.

192. ∾ A SYMPATHETIC WORLD

The world contains the potential for so much sympathy. Whatever the news may say, whatever your mind may say, your happiness is of great benefit to everyone—to all the men, women, and children who are waiting for you to flourish, whether they know it or not, as one candle waits to be lit by another. We all understand compassion in this timeless way—we always feel it somewhere in our hearts—and yet we often live according to the temporal order of self-pity, seeing our lives as a fall from youth into old age, from vitality into death, from importance into invisibility, from freedom into stress. How many times have you thought: *I remember being that happy, once, when I was younger?* But try to understand that there are many kinds of time, just as there are many radio frequencies, and you have a choice about which to tune your mind to right now. Whenever you feel unloved or uncared for, picture yourself at some moment in the past when you were truly happy. Picture yourself smiling or playing or resting at ease, and try to feel in your heart the deep wish that you have that you would always be that happy.

And then, as you feel your heart vibrating in tune with that wish, remind yourself that what you are feeling is right here, intact, incapable of being destroyed because it was never created in the first place. And as you open your eyes and carry this timeless compassion back into the world, remind yourself that you don't need to force or extract sympathy from anyone ever, for right here in your heart, sympathy was never missing in the first place.

193. ∾ THE HARVEST OF RESENTMENT

There is no life more beautiful than one that is free from resentment. No amount of wealth or status or privilege can compare with the feeling of being able to walk down a street without begrudging anyone or anything. If we truly understood this, we would pay less attention to the content of our thoughts—all those stories we tell ourselves about who did this or said that to us—and more to the intentions underlying those thoughts, intentions that, right now, are leading us either deeper into resentment, or away from it, into love. Bitter thoughts about the unfairness of the world lead to bitterness, not justice. Competitive thoughts about the superiority of our own lives lead to competition, not better living. And so it is that the best kinds of thoughts are thoughts of forgiveness: forgiveness for those who have hurt us, and forgiveness for ourselves for all the ways we have let ourselves down. Forgiveness works on the level of intention, not on the level of content, which means it has nothing to do with accepting or condoning the past and everything to do with preparing for the future that is rapidly coming. All the conflicts, disagreements, and pains you are feeling right now are passing from your life more quickly than you can imagine, and what you will inherit tomorrow is nothing but the reflection of the mind you cultivate today.

194. ∾ HUNGER STRIKES

Our resistance to having compassion for ourselves is often a way of protesting our mistreatment at the hands of others: parents, lovers, society in general. In this, we are like a man who leaves his house without a winter coat in order to protest winter. Though you can wage a hunger strike for the sake of an ideal, you cannot starve the heart for the sake of the heart.

195. ∾ A PLACE AT THE TABLE

Forgiveness, like all true generosity, comes from seeing that you have enough to give away, for you have a great wealth within you that cannot be diminished by anyone else's actions. Imagine that, on the last day of your life, you threw a banquet for everyone you had ever met. Imagine all the guests at one long table, stretching infinitely in both directions, with enough food and drink to satisfy everyone. And now imagine that even those who have hurt you have arrived, and imagine yourself seating them (far from you, of course) as you say, "Yes, there is room for you at my table. There is too much love here for you to hurt me or for me to hold love from you." That is forgiveness: not a feeling of obligation to interact with or be close to any of these difficult guests, but the realization that with all you have—all that space and abundance at the table of your heart—there is no reason to deny entry to anyone. The more you understand the limitlessness of your goodwill, the more you will naturally forgive, without hypocrisy or struggle. So today and every day, open your heart to those it is easiest to open to, but understand that this opening has no limit. If you follow it day after day, it will encompass everything and everyone that has made your life what it is.

196. ⚬ The Train You Are Waiting For

There is a train you are waiting for that is never going to come. Maybe it's fame; maybe it's a certain relationship; maybe it's money. It doesn't matter. Whoever you are, you deserve to be great—you deserve to live a life that is rare and beautiful—and yet, you must understand that what stands between you and your greatness is the fact that you have not yet mourned the death of some ideal. Whoever you are, seek out what you still hope will come save you and let yourself fully grieve for it, for it is only by grieving that you will learn how to find a deeper, more dependable happiness. Right now, you stand like a novice chef in front of a fully stocked refrigerator: you don't need any more ingredients, just more skill in putting them together. You have, in fact, already felt all the feelings there are—all the love, joy, pride, and exultation this life can offer—but you have not yet learned how to hold these things with a steady mind. And that is why you must practice gratitude, each and every day, for your life exactly as it is right now. Take time not only to count your blessings, but also to see that focusing on one blessing makes you aware of more and more blessings, till your life shines with a full and real goodness. For the irony is this: when you can love your life unconditionally, without needing anything in it to change, then everything in it will change for the better.

197. ⚬ Thistles in an Open Field

You don't have to make peace with the past, for the past is no longer there. You only have to make peace with yourself. What keeps you from moving forward in this life is not disappointment, which comes to us all, but your habit of feeding on that disappointment, of trying to draw sustenance from it although it poisons you. This is why we must practice forgiveness: not to embrace those who have hurt us, but to drag our resentments out into the light so we can see how toxic they are and develop distaste for them. So take some time today to clean your inner house. Call difficult people to mind, one by one, regardless of whether you can articulate the exact harm they have done you, and try to extend each your forgiveness. Understand, above all, that the ways we disappoint one another are as numerous and as natural as thistles in an open field, and that like the thistles, disappointments harm us only when we try to find nourishment in them. Don't worry so much about fixing all your relationships, for there is no end to that sort of work. Just keep feeling the weight of the burdens you have been carrying, and in time you will find the strength to put them down.

198. ❧ PULLING OUT THE SPLINTER

Sometimes you have to think about your problems. A lot of New Age spirituality tells us that we should never focus on what is negative, but if you never focus on what is negative, how will you ever learn from the past? The problem is not that we think too much, but rather that we think in a way that inflates and distorts our suffering, like a puppeteer who holds his shadow puppets up to the fire so that they casts huge, scary monsters on the wall. The way to stop the drama in your mind is not to stop thinking, but to see that your troubles are more like infections that form around a splinter: their sources are usually quite small, but through ignorance, we allow them to fester and swell. So today, when you find yourself in a dark mood all of a sudden, ask yourself: "At what precise moment did the darkness enter?" If you use your memory skillfully, the way you would use tweezers to remove a sliver beneath the surface of your skin, you will find your thinking to be a great tool, and you will start to develop confidence in your ability to heal yourself. For the truth is, you can travel this whole world in search of healing, but you will never find a more skillful doctor than your own well-trained mind.

199. ∾ A MIND THAT DOESN'T FLINCH

You're going to have to fight, you know. We talk too much about acceptance, and not nearly enough about pushing back against the darkness in our minds. You can call the darkness whatever you like—depression, the devil, childhood conditioning—but at some point, some shadowy part of your mind is going to take a swing at you. And when it does, if you look closely, you will see a desire in you to want to shut your eyes and just wait for the blows to rain down. Don't do that. Whatever thoughts of self-loathing or self doubt arise in you today, try to face them with open eyes and with a mind that doesn't flinch. That's really the hardest part. If you can keep your eyes open, you will quickly learn that your opponent isn't actually everywhere at once: he has his weaknesses, clumsy moves, holes in his guard. And as with most bullies, once you shove him back a few feet the first time, there may never be a need for a second confrontation.

200. ∾ DELIGHT IN SUFFERING

Until we see the delight we take in our suffering, we can't ever move past it. The mind is in many ways like a jealous lover who goes on his ex's Facebook page "to see what she's been up to." It isn't entirely correct to say he doesn't want to see her with another man, because, of course, no one forced him to lurk there on her page. And in the same way, it isn't entirely correct to say that we don't like thinking our painful thoughts, for in reality, no one forces us to dwell on our anxieties, resentments, and various forms of self-hatred. There is part of the mind that delights in this painful thinking, partly because it believes, in doing so, it can control the past. The Thai ajaans say this kind of thinking is like "a dog chewing on old bones": the dog thinks it's getting a new chance at a new meal, but really it's just tasting the taste of its own saliva. And so, in order to move past what is keeping you stuck, you have to look squarely at this tendency of the mind to delight in suffering and not get discouraged by it. Today, when old patterns of jealousy, anger, or self-hatred arise, don't try to "wallpaper" over these patterns with insincere affirmations of self-worth. It's more important to become disillusioned with how you've been thinking than to prop yourself up with cheap words. We don't learn not to touch a hot stove by telling ourselves how smart or likable or good we are. We learn not to touch a hot stove by feeling the burn and moving effortlessly in the opposite direction. Pain leads us to faith in ourselves, faith leads us to joy, and joy leads us, in the end, to peace.

201. ∾ OCCUPY YOUR PERCEPTIONS

Learn to occupy your perceptions. In your mind, decisions are being made for you every moment, without your consent, or rather, with as much consent as you choose to assert. When you get angry, for example, you may perceive that there is a pressure inside you that only aggression will release, but that perception only seems inevitable because you don't fully inhabit it within your body. Your consciousness is somewhere else, lost in thought, perhaps, when the laws that seem to govern your emotions are being drafted. The truth is, you could perceive your anger differently: as a soft heat radiating from your pores, or an energy flowing through your arms and legs. You don't have to control or stifle anything you feel. Just exercise your freedom of perception, which, as with all freedoms, demands that you be there to use it.

202. ∾ WHAT CALLS FOR YOUR ATTENTION

How much time do you need to spend with your sadness? Only you can know. But as my teacher says, we must learn to listen for the thoughts that are genuinely calling for our attention, rather than the ones that are just calling out at random. Some sadnesses know you by name, like old friends who have crossed great distances to tell you something important or apologize for what happened long ago. Some sadnesses are like that, but you won't recognize them till you see that most sad thoughts are just like hawkers in the street who care only about grabbing your attention, not about loving or healing you. And even many of our well-intentioned sad thoughts are like those activists who stop you in parks to say, "Sir, don't you care about the environment?" "Sir, don't you care about what's happening to our world?" And of course the answer is, yes, you care very much, but you have only one life to live, and you will never live it, let alone get to the other side of the park, if you keep letting yourself get stopped. And so it is with sadness, whose urgency, we must learn, is not always our urgency. So the next time sadness grips you, remind yourself, "Any insight that is true can wait." For this is a feature of wisdom we often forget: it waits. Wisdom is what remains true even when you don't think about it all the time. It is the old friend who comes into the cafe after all these years, sits down with a smile that hasn't changed, and says, "Well, better late than never."

203. ∾ BAND-AIDS FALL OFF ON THEIR OWN
It's not helpful to tell someone in pain, "Let go." First of all, that's the wrong image: suffering doesn't come from something you're holding; it comes from something you're doing. And no matter how much you try to let go of your pain, you will keep doing what you're doing the exact same way until you realize there's another way of doing it. That other way, basically, is with love. So if you must give advice, say, "Try to meet your experience with love, and everything else will be okay." Just that. No more talk about ripping off the Band-Aid. Everyone knows Band-Aids fall off on their own. The point is to stop wounding ourselves.

204. ❧ Peeling Back the Onion

You have to deal with the top layer of your difficulties first. You can't face your fears if you're angry about having fears. You can't face your anger if you doubt your ability to survive it. Very often, the top layer of a difficulty is a sense of shame that we have problems at all. My experience is that, as with an onion, this outermost skin is hardest to peel, but the inner layers unravel with surprising ease. Either way, layer by layer, the whole thing comes apart in time.

205. ❧ The Yielding Point of Experience

What seems to be resistance around us is mostly resentment within us. For life never opposes anyone; in fact, it flows easily around most difficulties, as a stream flows easily around even the largest rocks. It is the mind that collides head on with its own grudges and grievances. This is why we need to practice forgiveness: not merely to be kind, but to find the yielding point of our experience.

206. ❧ Everybody Hurts

You want to feel loved. But feeling loved is not a matter of enough attention or affection, it is a matter of understanding that everybody hurts the same way. Sickness, aging, death, separation: these things are universal. We face them together, rich and the poor alike, and even between the wise and the foolish there is only a hair's breadth of difference in awareness of these truths. So to feel truly touched by another human being in this life is to risk the idea that your pain and heartbreak are not unprecedented in human history, that they have in fact already been felt by everyone who has ever lived. Without this awareness, no one really touches anyone—life is just bodies colliding in the dark. So as you walk through the streets today, search for your struggles in the eyes of those you pass, and wish these strangers freedom from the pain that is also yours. And then see if, somehow, you don't feel a bit more loved, without any embrace, without any conversation, but only with the presence of a kindness that is always everywhere.

207. ∾ What Hides behind Fear
People aspire to being fearless, but fear itself is neither good nor bad. The problem is what hides behind fear: usually some form of self-doubt, self-hatred, or self-importance. On its own, fear is just a searchlight, the body's way of directing attention to something important. The trouble comes when we grab hold of the light the wrong way, blinding ourselves and letting our worst impulses take over in the confusion. So when fear comes, don't resist or clamp down on it, but allow the feeling of adrenalin to spread freely throughout your body. If you can do this, you will find fear can coexist with great calm, confidence, and even wisdom.

208. ∾ Homesick for the Present
When you do what you love, you will always feel a little inadequate. Learn to regard this sense of incompleteness not as a sign of failure, but as a sign of metamorphosis, and embrace it with your whole life. Live so that if a genie were to transport you back to your past accomplishments, you would feel nothing but homesickness for your present difficulties.

209. ∾ Picturing Is the First Step to Feeling
Beneath so many of our ruts and repetitions is a desire to be thought well of by those who have hurt us. And even anger, which seems at first like a way of cutting ties with our abusers, still keeps us fixed to wanting someone else's good opinion. Only love puts an end to these pointless desires—love, not in the sense of pleasing or being pleased, but in the sense of wishing all people well from a distance. You must

search your mind every day for those you still resent, and one by one, picture them all at peace, at ease, understanding that they, like you, are just fumbling for happiness in the dark. Don't worry if what you picture doesn't yet have a place in reality. Picturing is the first step to feeling, and feeling is the first step to letting go.

210. ∾ Put on Your Coat

It's hard to be happy when you see every resistance in life as the mark of some inner flaw. If what healing means to you is fixing things up so you don't have to deal with a defiant world and a defiant heart, you will surely hurt yourself more. If resistance is evidence of anything, it's evidence of needing to take better care of yourself. You don't have to work so hard to keep the wind from blowing. In other words: just put on your coat.

211. ∾ I Haven't Figured Out How That Works Yet

Don't worry so much about what your life looks like. Beneath so much modern talk about "manifesting" this or that dream, there still lies the old Protestant idea that you are only worth as much as you can prove to the world. If you really want to be happy, you have to resist that idea, each and every day, for it will keep you from making the most you of your life. You must remember that, at any given moment, you are "manifesting" far more than you could possibly understand or keep up with. Like a teenager who doesn't yet know her own strength, you have more power and less control than you think. So while a part of your life must involve striving to do your best, another equally important part must involve developing an inner refuge where you can be safe from the unintended consequences of what you have not yet mastered. You are going to do the wrong thing, say the wrong thing, and above all, think the wrong thing at times. But your safe haven in all of this lies in remembering your basic worthiness, the basic fact that you deserve to be well, to be happy, to flourish. So when something in your life doesn't match your expectations, just tell yourself, "Okay, I guess I haven't figured out how that works yet." No one faults a kid who hasn't taken piano lessons for not already being a virtuoso, so don't fault yourself, who have yet to live your whole life, for not already having mastered it.

212. ∽ THE FALL

In so many of us, there is a sense of having fallen. In so many of us, there is the thought: I was better back then, back when I was younger. Better at living, better at loving. What happened to my light? Of course, we know on some level that these thoughts aren't true in any real sense, but because we are in such a hurry to push away the panic and reassure ourselves that our lives are now better than ever, we miss the point of our fears about aging. When moments of nostalgia overwhelm you, when you fear that joys you once had are gone forever, these moments are trying to show you something: not that your life is over, but that you must begin again; not that the years are a downward slope, but that they are a spiral returning you to the same spot in order that you may go deeper this time around. And so, you must treat every happy thought about the past as a reminder of something you have forgotten, something precious and eternal that is still right here in the present moment. Stop beating yourself up that you have lost the thread of what is important. Of course you have forgotten, and of course you will remember once again. You have not fallen, any more than everything in this life is falling. But you still have time to see the still point beyond the fall.

213. ∽ NO, THANK YOU

We often confuse disenchantment with depression. When we aren't satisfied by the little trinkets life tosses at our feet, we fear this discontent may be a sign of some illness. But in the end, nothing makes us more depressed than over-enchantment with this world. So don't fear your disillusionment, but guide it toward something truly beautiful. The trick is learning to say, "No, thank you" without a trace of resentment in your heart.

214. ∿ JAMMING THE TRANSMISSION

The only way to find the truth is to become more truthful. Like radio waves, the truth is always there—the truth of what you feel, where you are going in this life, what is calling you on—but your inner instrument is often not yet sensitive enough to pick up the signal. One way we jam the transmission of truth is by failing to keep to our word. When we overschedule, for example, thinking, *I'll make that appointment but probably won't keep it*, we allow our focus on what is real to blur, and it is therefore blurriness that we find when we turn to look inside. So today, try to keep your commitments, however unpleasant they might seem. If you promised to do something and wish you hadn't, remind yourself that by being true to what you said you are tuning in to a deeper communication that is guiding you somewhere better. Keep tuning in, keep listening, keep taking joy in your ability to show up. For there are few inconveniences that are not well worth the ability to hear your inner voice, loud and clear, above the din and chaos of this unreliable world.

215. ∿ LISTEN TO YOUR INTUITION

Listen to your intuition. The problem isn't that you have intuitions, but rather, that you defend or dismiss them before you have a chance to see where they actually lead. If something inside you makes you not want to cross a street, then don't cross that street. But rather than telling yourself a long story about how crazy you are, or that you have been gifted with powers that set you apart from the rest of the human race, take some time to watch what happens next: perhaps the bad feeling you had will turn out to have come from the last thought you were thinking; perhaps it will prove to be nothing more than the residue of sadness you picked up from the old man standing next to you on the sidewalk. You have to test your powers in order to develop them, and you have to be willing to be wrong. For the whole world runs on intuition—generals launch missile strikes based on intuition, people get married and divorced based on intuition— and there's nothing evolved about any of this, except in the rare cases where people are willing to be truthful and observant about what's in their minds. So today, see if you can pay attention to the subtle feelings that arise in your body in connection with what is happening around you, and see if you can listen to these sensations in a way that neither wants to believe nor reject them, but only understand them. Let your consciousness be like a field of wheat in the wind that tells no story about where and why the breezes blow, but only bends according to the currents passing through it. For the deepest proof of your intuition is nothing you could say or think, but only how you respond to life.

216. ❧ Unripe Mercy

Resist the urge to forgive prematurely, for unripe mercy is a benefit to no one. Try instead to picture those who have hurt you doing something kind or generous. It doesn't matter if they ever will act this way; the image itself can give you the dispassion you need to move on. At very least, it will show you the limits of your imagination.

217. ❧ You're Not on a Witness Stand

Truthfulness depends on understanding that you don't have to answer every question that is put to you. Part of the reason we tell lies in the first place is that we don't feel any barrier between ourselves and other people's expectations. And of course, the more we lie, the less protected and more dependent on what others think we end up feeling. So in order to break this cycle, we have to learn that we are not sensors that must light up with a response whenever our buttons are pressed. This often means learning some very practical skills: how to change a subject, how to answer a different question, how to find the space between a question and a need for an answer.

218. ∾ THE RAFT OF GENEROSITY

In the sea of every heartbreak, you will find the raft of your own generosity. And you will be surprised again how life delivers you: not just by the help of others, but by helping others. For what we think is the issue is rarely the issue, and what we think is the thorn in our chests is rarely the thorn. And all of pain exists to point to this truth: that if you purify your intentions, you will be happy in this life. We learn this first by showing up for others that we may learn to show up for ourselves. So today, try to help someone, and later, when you are alone again with your pain, reflect that your generosity still is there. Without reaching for your wallet or even for anyone else, ask yourself, "What can I give to this moment?" And you will see just how much you have to give.

219. ∾ STITCH BY STITCH

Life doesn't listen to what you say, it listens to what you mean. If you tell flattering stories about yourself in order to defend against what is difficult in your experience, your life will only grow in the direction of defensiveness, and you will find yourself more and more at odds with what is happening. This doesn't mean you have to just sit there and let the darkness take over your mind. It means that when you're not feeling great, you have to remind yourself that your life is not a test, not something you have to justify, and that what you think the "score" is matters less than what you are actually learning. Think of your state of mind as something you are knitting: if you drop a stitch, it won't do any good to keep pushing ahead—you eventually will need to unravel the whole thing and start again. But in every mood, there is something that cannot be unraveled: your wisdom and your skill, both of which are steadily growing, no matter how great or small your sense of wellbeing is. So the next time you find yourself trying to tell yourself, "I'm okay," tell yourself instead, "I have what it takes to be happy, even if I don't feel that way right now." And then start again, stitch by stitch, building up your state of mind by focusing on your blessings, and on what feels good. Wherever you are, just pick up the thread; it is right there in your hands, where it has always been.

220. ∾ COMING INTO TUNE

You will be lonely sometimes, but try to see your loneliness not as the silencing of your soul, but as the process of coming into tune with it. For life draws us inward not to keep its music from us, but to make us better instruments on which that music can be played.

221. ∾ ALONE TOGETHER

Don't take your loneliness so personally: you share it with everyone who has ever lived. Loneliness is often the last step before love, just as the darkest hour comes right before the dawn, and the trouble is not that you get lonely, but that you flee from your loneliness into the deeper darkness of your own house, from which you never get to see the sun rise. What is loneliness but a longing for something greater than yourself? It is something greater than ordinary human contact, greater than all the daily issues of whether this person will call you back or that person will say the right words of affection. And if you can sit with that longing long enough, you will find that its fulfillment has always been right here within you, waiting only on your own sensitivity to flower. But to develop that sensitivity, you must first understand that you are in fact not alone, that we are all in this together, trying, in our separate ways, to find a happiness that can neither be created nor be destroyed by anyone or anything. So today, when your mind gets dark, go for a walk, and as you pass people in the streets, remind yourself that they, like you, have a wish to be happy. They, like you, are searching for an intimacy that is greater than the sum of their partners. Rest your burden in the eyes of these strangers. There is no one who cannot comfort you.

222. ∾ Fixing and Healing

The work of healing is not the work of fixing, though we often confuse the two. There are many problems in life that can't be fixed: aging, death, and separation, to name just a few. Healing does not come from repairing any of these things, but from learning how to occupy the role of the observer in our lives. For when we watch over our minds and actions from a loving distance, we begin to know a sense of ease, security, and intimacy with ourselves and our surroundings, and our lives take on a wholeness that does not depend on mending any of the broken pieces within it. We often look to the fixing mind to bring us closer to life, but it usually accomplishes the opposite, just as a camera held too close fails to capture the beauty of its subject. So when troubles come to you today, fix those you can, but make sure not to let that fixing interfere with the deeper work of your healing.

223. ∾ Evolution Through Pain

Frustration is a form of guidance. In the biological world, the ability to feel pain only increases with evolution and is actually a requirement for higher forms of learning. Yet in our emotional lives, we tend to see discontent as a disorder, and we try to blot out the signals it sends us rather than trace them to their source. The irony is that this is why we need to practice gratitude every day, for gratitude is not, as some people think, a way of pretending everything is fine, but rather, a way of understanding what isn't working by focusing on what is. The great danger in life is not that we will feel pain, but that our pain will become so indistinguishable from the rest of our experience that we will no longer be able to find any information in it. So spend some time today counting your blessings. Call to mind what is thriving in your body, work, and relationships. Be clear about which flowers you are growing before you start trying to weed your garden. Without gratitude, your plans for self-improvement will always end in disappointment, but with a grateful heart, the reverse is true: every disappointment leads to self-improvement.

224. ∾ INTERNET TROLLS

You don't have to be so afraid of your negative thoughts. It is true that how you think determines your happiness, but people often develop a contagion phobia about negativity, as though it were a deadly virus that could ravage their lives after just a brief moment of exposure. You are stronger than that. At some point, you are going to pick up some negative thoughts, just as you are going to pick up some germs, and the key to a healthy immune system in either case is not to quarantine yourself, but to understand what you are carrying. The germs of worry, anger, and self-loathing cannot survive in your mind unless you nurture them with your internal dialogue—just like those Internet trolls whose nasty comments cannot survive without the thread of someone else's conversation. Our problem is we think we have to feed the trolls, as though we would be standing in the way of free speech or human progress if we didn't. So today, when your mind gets dark, remind yourself that it's your inner conversation, and your choice about who gets to participate. If some inconvenient truth needs to be revealed to you, it will be revealed in a kind tone of voice. Don't try to reason or argue with your negativity, and don't judge yourself for it. It is actually a sign that you are getting stronger and healthier, for what is strong and healthy always attracts parasites. But as soon as you see them clearly, they will release their jaws.

225. ∾ RESTRAINT AND REPRESSION

Learn the difference between restraint and repression. Your feelings are little children: not yet ready to run your life, and yet they are its future. If you repress them, they will fight you and overpower you one day. You must restrain them now, for restraint is a way of protecting them, of letting them express in innocence what they would be punished for in action. There are going be people who stir up "irrational" emotions in you. Try not to get upset by the unreasonableness of these feelings, for then you will have lost the battle for tomorrow. Take out a sheet of paper and give free reign to your resentments there, within the safety of a page you will never show to anyone. So much of our growth is like an unsent letter, whose purpose, we discover only later, is not to make a point but to learn how to let go of one.

226. ∾ IT'S JUST INFORMATION

You cannot change a feeling, not your own or anyone else's. Understanding this is the first step in developing self-respect. We are always saying things like, "He disrespected me," by which we mean that someone did something we don't like, and now we have feelings we don't want and are waiting for the other person to take those feelings away. Most human conflict, in fact, doesn't come directly from anger, but from the belief that we cannot survive our own anger unless we force others to take responsibility for it. This is the ultimate form of self-disrespect, for our inability to tolerate our own difficult emotions is essentially an inability to tolerate ourselves as we actually are. So today, when someone stirs up some strong feeling in you, remind yourself, "That's just information. I don't necessarily need to do anything with it." Try to act as a leader within the committee of your own mind, listening to all points of view but not allowing yourself to be bullied into following any of them. If you can't find that kind of sovereignty within your own being, you will not find it in the way others treat you.

227. ❧ MICROBES OF BLINDNESS

When someone lashes out at you, treat her as you would treat a person suffering from a fever: keep distance, but wish her a speedy recovery and don't take her condition personally. For anger is really a sort of infection, an invasion of body and mind by microbes of blindness. This should inspire in us a sense of kinship with each other. Healthy people see the sick and understand their own potential for illness. Sick people, on the other hand, forget that we are mirrors of each other, and gazing into the reflections they find in others, believe in their delirium that they are better than what they see.

228. ❧ JUST FOR TODAY

You don't have to let your sorrows go. Just let your sorrows be. As Ram Dass said, a snake doesn't shed its skin all at once: it goes around for a while with the old skin half on. And you, too, are going to go around for a while with your old skin half on. It doesn't matter. What counts is only that you find a little ease, a little love for yourself in the midst of your molting state. And how do you that? Not by trying to cut away the past or frantically seek an alternative future, but by letting the words "just for today" sink into your heart and being. Just for today, maybe you can go where the warmth is, allowing friends and teachers to hold you in their loving concern. Just for today, maybe you can feel your pain as a question for which no answer has yet come into being. Just for today, maybe you can do something and put down the burden of having to do everything. This life you are so anxiously trying to perfect is no more than a string of todays. So pass through this day with as much love and grace as you can manage, and know that is enough.

229. ∾ THE NOISE OF LONELINESS

You must protect your solitude, not just from the noise of the world, but also from the forces of loneliness that seek to destroy your solitude from within. I remember talking once with the abbot of a monastery, who surprised me by saying how much he disapproved of monks going off to caves to meditate. We need each other, he said, to make sense of what we discover when we are alone, and too much isolation only brings danger to the mind. When I look back on my childhood solitude, I see how much I learned about imagination and self-reliance, but I see also how much time I spent feeding a beast that, to this day, rises up whenever I'm alone and threatens to overthrow the beauty of my aloneness with another feeling: the feeling of being unloved and unlovable. It is for this reason that we can never choose between solitude and relationships, for neither really exists without the other. So today, try to be conscious about this interplay. Go for a walk or spend some time by yourself, and then call or see a friend afterwards. You don't have to discuss your solitude with that friend, but notice how togetherness and separateness bring each other into balance. That balance is an essential part of love.

230. ～ A Thin Skin Means You're Living Closer to the Future

It's okay to have a thin skin. A thin skin means you are living closer to the future, for when you are sensitive to what you don't like about your life right now, you are that much more in touch with what you ultimately want. A greater ability to tolerate pain often indicates a smaller, more mediocre vision of what life is capable of being. So never lose your sensitivity and keep dreaming big. Only make sure that your sensitivity is coupled with a different kind of strength—not the strength of endurance, but the strength of remembering that your happiness depends on your own actions, not on other people's behavior or on perfect circumstances. If people let you down, don't say you are disappointed in them; rather, say that there is disappointment within you guiding you toward the life you have always desired. Try to develop the perception that the sorrow and pain you are feeling are not coming at you, but instead are coming up in order to leave you, and face them like a kid sitting in a backwards-facing carseat, waving goodbye to the road that rolls out behind her. For in the end, sensitivity is really just sensitivity to what you must one day leave. So today, instead of getting irritated with yourself for being irritated, or upset with yourself for being upset, try to honor what you are feeling and follow it toward a deeper, more compassionate equanimity. You have what it takes to feel it all and still lead a joyful life.

231. ～ Pacific Fogs

Anger is an imprecise emotion. It means many things, which is why it confuses us. We often explore anger when we ought to turn away from it, and just as often we turn away from it when we ought to explore it. Anger is a strong wind that, in the hands of an inexperienced sailor, can overturn a boat, but in the hands of a veteran can provide the energy to move forward. Ill will, on the other hand, is much simpler: If you wish others harm, it will destroy your happiness, so fight that impulse with all your might. Ill will is like those dense Pacific fogs that no one can see or move through. If you find yourself caught in it, you must stop everything and keep still till it passes. With caution, you can navigate anger, perhaps, but you will never pass through ill will unharmed.

232. ∽ CHEEKY PUPPETS

No one can ever judge you as harshly as you judge yourself. We spend so much of our lives silently defending ourselves against what we imagine to be the accusations of others that we forget all these voices are really our own—like some ventriloquist show where the puppet insults the puppeteer. But when you see that the whole spectacle exists only in your mind, when you see that you are the one pulling the strings of this feeling of being condemned, you can begin to release your puppets, like that fairytale where the marionettes come to life and dance their way off stage. Let them exit. Without them, you are loved more than you could possibly imagine.

233. ∽ A HERO'S STORY

Try to make your problems count. We are beings who have problems, as no one needs to be reminded, and what we often forget is that our problems are what give our lives shape and significance, and what make them more than a mindless stretch of days passing into oblivion. So the problem is not that we have problems, but that our problems are not yet great and meaningful enough to make us proud, to inspire us. This is an area in which we have more control than we think. Whatever is troubling you today—a conflict with a friend, family member, or coworker, perhaps—see if you can tell the story in more heroic terms. Instead of focusing on the narrow-minded details of who did or said what, or denying the conflict entirely, see if you can feel how difficult your struggle with resentment has been, how long this struggle has been going on, and the nobility of your continued resistance to the darker forces in your mind. For in the end, to love yourself truly is to love the greatness within you; your work is not to remove discomfort from your life, but to keep yourself from pettiness, no matter how great the suffering.

234. ∾ POSSESSION

Pay attention to the moments when you feel your life is going nowhere. Resist the urge to sweep these moments aside or reassure yourself that everything is okay. You have to learn, on a level deeper than words, that doubt is a kind of possession, like a demon that takes over your mind and speaks with your mouth. If that sounds overly dramatic or superstitious, ask yourself, "Whose voice is this doubt?" If you really listen, you will see that it is not your own: it belongs to your father or mother or an ex-lover or a playground bully from the fourth grade. Whatever the case, you must remember that doubt derives its power from your habit of identifying with your aggressors, past and present. If a random person on the street told you that your life was going nowhere, you'd just keep walking, but because you are still trying to redeem these old figures of authority, you keep thinking that you are your doubt. And so you must learn to watch this drama rather than take part in it, to keep still and not struggle so hard to make "something" of your life. For when you are free from doubt, walking down the street will be enough, sitting quietly will be enough, and you will find your life is moving without having to make a move—what the Taoists call "heaven within a mountain."

235. ∾ REAL PREDATORS

Your mind is not bad any more than a jungle is bad. Yet there are real predators in both.

236. ∾ THE MIND'S IMMUNE SYSTEM

The mind has its immune system just as the body does. Remember this next time you find yourself struggling in some area of your life. It is neither possible nor helpful to quarantine yourself from everything that is coming at you right now. You have to develop a healthy response to your troubles that comes from within. We build immunity in our minds the same way we build it in our bodies: by introducing the germ of the problem on a very small scale and letting ourselves adapt to it slowly. To do this, you need to learn how to acknowledge a problem once and then put it off to the side, focusing instead on your breath, your body, or your blessings. You don't need to rid your surroundings of disease or go off and live in a bubble. You have great power to heal yourself where you are, if only you get out of your own way.

237. ∾ DON'T LET YOURSELF OFF THE HOOK

Don't be so tolerant of your low self-esteem. One of the main functions of the discouraging words you tell yourself all day long is to let you off the hook: if you're no good, you see, then you don't have to try. Realizing this should spark in you a sense of righteous indignation, a sense that, actually, there is something good growing in your garden, something you are determined to protect at all costs. Take a walk today, and as you walk, make up your mind that you will only think thoughts of gratitude. You can reflect on the good people and good circumstances in your life, or the goodness in the world around you. Then gradually, try to shift your awareness to the good qualities within you: your patience, persistence, sense of humor. Notice how you feel after walking and counting your blessings. If you look closely, you should see the flowering of your gratitude in some small way. And once you see that, once you see that you really do have the power to make things grow, you really have no choice but to try to make them thrive.

238. ∽ A SENSE OF ADVENTURE

Try to have a sense of adventure about what is most difficult in your heart. You do not travel to a foreign country in order to be comfortable, but in order to be stripped of your usual sense of self. In the same way, your inner awareness always travels toward what breaks you down, not what is easy. And so you must learn to resist the humiliation that often accompanies difficult emotions, that sense of, "Why is this happening to me?" When sadness arises, or any other kind of pain, you must remind yourself, "What have I come here for, if not to see what I haven't yet seen, to become who I haven't yet become?" Don't be like those travelers who only talk about how things were better back at home or how one country resembles another. Right here at the center of your heart, in pathways you haven't walked before filled with voices you don't yet understand, something new is being shown to you. Embrace it, and be thankful you never asked to live an ordinary life.

239. ∽ MURDEROUS HOUSE CATS

If you want to make peace with your difficult emotions, you're going to have to acknowledge their service to you. Anger, jealousy, and resentment are like house cats constantly dragging bloody, disagreeable things into your life. But if you yell at a cat for bringing in a mouse, the cat will think you are upset about the quality of its prey, and will bring you bigger, better game from its next hunt. So if you want to train the cat, you have to praise its hunting prowess, even as you deposit the kill outside the door. The same is true of your difficult emotions, all of which came into being to serve and protect you. And so you must thank each impulse, even as you separate it from its object. You can appreciate anger, for example, as an energy in your body without letting it drag dangerous situations into your life. All too often, we become aware of difficult emotions only because of the difficult people they attract, and we ask, "Why is the world against me?" But the fault doesn't lie in the world or even in your own failings as a human being, but in the fact that part of you is still hunting for trouble, trying to prove itself. So seek that part out, and be to it what a mother is to her child: patient with what is still untaught, yet grateful to be custodian of so much beautiful wildness.

240. ✎ FREEDOM TO BE WRONG

Among our most precious freedoms is the freedom to be wrong. In moments of being wrong, we have an opportunity to rediscover the freshness of the world and the relief, actually, that life is bigger than our views of it. So today, when you make a mistake, try to muster up the courage to tell someone about it. And when you find yourself fixated on the idea that others are wrong, ask yourself whether the energy it takes to construe their actions in a certain way or their words according to a certain meaning is actually serving you. For you, above all, deserve to be at ease, and to be free from the tiresome condition of needing to be right. You don't need to sink into guilt; cowering like a dog on its back is no use to anyone. Just notice the way that, by admitting your errors and what you have left to learn, your awareness broadens. Take joy in that expansion.

241. ✎ BULLIES

We all have our addictions. It's important to be clear about the ones you have, and just as important, to be clear about the ones you don't.

We tend to measure addiction according to what other people think of our behavior, and this is why we are so often lost in guilt about things that do no harm at all and complacent about harm that is socially acceptable. If you really want to find freedom in your life, you have to realize that the majority of your life consists of mental actions, not physical ones, and so in the end, you have to judge your addictions on the basis of the amount of craving and clinging within your own mind. Just as some people can't have one drink without already craving the next one, other people can't have a little attention without craving more attention, or a little guilt without craving more guilt, or a little anxiety without craving more anxiety. Addiction is fueled by the mind's habit of focusing on what it lacks rather than on what it has. And so you must make it a practice, every day, to notice when you are caught in focusing on the absence of what you want, and to understand the pain in that way of living. You must ask yourself, "How does this guilt/worry/insecurity feel?" and try to connect to your natural disgust for what, after all, is poisoning you. See if you can have a sense that enough is enough. For clinging and craving are like those bullies we once faced at school: they will keep pinning you to the ground, day after day, until you stand up for yourself.

242. ∾ THIS IS JUST A REUNION

You must learn to visit your sadness as you would visit any place from the past: without staying too long. The problem is not that you feel sad sometimes, but that you forget you are looking at a memory, just as someone who has coffee with an old lover might forget that he doesn't have to work things out with her any more or find a way to move back in. In the same way, too much intimacy with sadness can be just as false as too much distance. And so you must always remember to feel your breath, right here in the present moment, as one might feel an airplane ticket in her pocket and know that, whatever happens, she will be leaving soon. So today, when you feel some sadness creeping in, take a few deep breaths and remind yourself: "This is just a reunion." You can no more hold on to your sadness forever than you can hold on to a breath forever. Everything changes; everything gets released. Just feel the sadness in your body for a few moments, thank it for reminding you of where you come from, and then return to your real life, which is always now.

243. ∾ INSOMNIA

Overcoming heartbreak is a bit like overcoming insomnia. You have to forget about finding rest. You have to forget about letting go. Give yourself permission to stay up all night with your troubles. But find something pleasant in the present to put your attention on: the coolness of your pillow, the ease in your breath. That is your work. When the mind understands that peace is real, the rest of you will lay down your burden without effort.

244. ∾ MOURNING A DREAM

Mourning is a larger part of life than we imagine. Hopefully you will not have to mourn the deaths of too many loved ones, but you will certainly have to mourn the deaths of many of your dreams, and how you mourn these losses will be just as important in deciding whether you will be able to move forward in your life. For the most part, we are taught to forget whatever we cannot fix. When a desire for a certain career or relationship or way of life doesn't pan out, you will feel pressure to pretend that the dream never existed, or to move on to the next one. But this is how we repeat our mistakes, by not taking time to mourn what we cannot resolve. You must remember that, when a dream dies, you are on a boat sailing between two shores. You cannot turn back, but neither can you be on the other side just yet. You must embrace where you are on your voyage by feeling pain, but feeling it in such a way that you feel it receding: it is here and may be for a while, but not forever. Then the corpses of your disappointments start to break up, to dissolve, and to fertilize the soil for the greater beauty that is still to come.

245. ∾ SITTING BY A SICK BED

Your body is only yours the way a child can be yours: to love and to care for, but never to share a destiny with. Your body, like a child, is outgrowing you day by day, and many of the pains you feel are not due to some fault of yours, but only to the natural parting of your two paths. We forget this, the way we forget that our greatest human gift is compassion, not intervention. When a child is sick, you can try to make him better, but mostly he just needs someone to sit by his bed and remind him he's not alone. If only we could be with ourselves in this same way—the nights would not be so long, nor the pain separable from great joy.

246. ∾ THE MOLD OF RESENTMENT

Whatever you have to do today, try to do it without resentment. Like a mold in damp weather, resentment can grow on nearly anything and make you sick before you know it's there. Resentment thrives wherever your attention to what you dislike about the present outweighs your attention to what would actually make you happy. So often, words that appear wholesome actually harbor resentments in their secret "because" clauses. For example: "I would love to take a yoga class (because I resent myself for being so out of shape)" or "I would love to learn how to meditate (because I resent my mind for being such a mess)." If you don't learn to catch these resentments and root them out, every hill you climb will only remind you of all the mountains you are still at the foot of. So today, even with tasks you didn't choose, find a reason for them that is free of resentment. Tell yourself: "I am going to go to work . . . because it will feel good to have enough money to pay my bills" or "I am going to run errands at the store . . . because it will feel good to have a well-stocked home." If you practice this way, you will see that the content of your labor matters less than the intention behind it. Through the window of self-care, every passing experience, no matter how much toil or attention it takes, is pure and joyful.

247. ⌘ LONELY AGAIN FOR THE FIRST TIME

Let your loneliness in, for it has so much to teach you. Do you see that you feel most alone at moments of repetition, moments when something or someone leaves and you feel the weight of all the things and people that have ever left you? You must learn to treat these moments with care and not push them away, for it is by struggling against repetition that we bring it about—by acting in the same, desperate way we always have. When you feel lonely, remind yourself that you have an opportunity to do things differently this time around; you have an opportunity to heal in ways you have not yet let yourself. Understand, above all, that you are not lonely because you lack people, but because there is some part of yourself you have not yet accepted. Try to picture that part, in all its weakness, confusion, and fear, and bring it into alignment with the great love that exists within you. People always say, "I have so much love to give, and yet I'm alone." Well, draw on that love, feel it in your heart, and let it fuse what has been fractured within you, rather than wasting it on trying to make the surface of your life look a certain way. For just as a broken bone needs internal alignment, not external movement, in order to heal, the same is true of your heart. Keep still and let yourself receive the strength that is your birthright. Love is still there, for love is everywhere.

248. ∽ No More Russian Novels, Please

Life is complex enough, and we make it more so with our desire to put a stamp of originality on everything we experience. Someone says something you don't like and you draft elaborate testimonies to convince a hypothetical judge that this injustice stands out among all injustices. Your back hurts, but rather than face the pain directly, you write a long Russian novel in your head about how this moment signals your inevitable descent into old age and death. Your storytelling skills could be put to better use. As every writer learns, the less detail you give, the more room the reader has to fill that space with his own feelings. Compassion for yourself works the same way. If you can let unpleasant things be what they are without crowding your mind with their details, you will find space in your heart in which a true and tender love for yourself can grow. I once read an interview with Paul Simon in which he said that when he wants to write a sad song, he goes through his lyrics and deletes the saddest lines. Often, the compassion in a piece of art shines through only when the obvious darkness is subtracted. So today, think of your difficulties as an artist would. Try to see how much you can omit from the story you are telling. Beneath the dense overgrowth of your own perceived uniqueness, something simple, true, and joyful is flowering.

249. ∽ Nothing Has Broken

What we call heartbreak is not a breaking at all, but only the contraction of our awareness. For the truth is that we are loved from all directions: by the earth that feeds us, by the breath that sustains us, and by the wisdom that waits for us in all things. But because we so often experience love as a tightening of focus, a clenching of consciousness, we forget that when the narrow point of our affection disappears, we still have the ability to pull back the lens and behold the complete scope of love. You can learn a lot about

heartbreak by taking long walks, for as you move through streets or forests, upon the earth and under the sky, you will find your awareness naturally becoming as large as the world around you. And as you walk with this enlarged awareness, you will remember: Nothing in you has broken. Nothing has dried up. You are standing in a rainstorm of beauty and wonder. You don't have to keep gathering water with a eyedropper
.

250. ∾ KEEP MOVING

In sadness, we are often like those who, dying of the cold, suddenly feel a warmth in their bodies that makes them want to sleep. This is our most dangerous impulse: to lie down with our troubles and lose consciousness with them. We have to keep moving. When darkness comes, take walks, talk with friends, above all, count your blessings. It is only when we've reached shelter that we can deal with our wounds.

251. ∾ STILLNESS IS MEDICINE

Stillness is medicine. What keeps us from slowing down is not our schedules but our lack of faith in the healing properties of silence. If we could learn to feel stillness doing its work on us, as one might feel aloe seeping into a sunburn, we would seek stillness in more and more of our lives. Be careful, then, about judging yourself for being busy, for judgment makes you cling to being busy even more. If all you have today are five minutes to take a walk, make the most of them. Soak up the quiet moments and they will multiply, like patches of blue sky when the clouds soak up the sun.

252. ∾ A PROPER NAP

Learn how to take a proper nap. Seriously. We so often associate napping with laziness, indulgence, or avoidance that we forget the healing effect that a nap can have on the mind. Like the clutch on an old-fashioned car, a nap disengages the gears of your mind and slows down the momentum of your painful thoughts. You may tell yourself that your weariness comes from having too much work, but the greater part of your exhaustion comes from being caught in a trajectory of thinking that you don't have the strength to resist. So the next time you feel weary and have a few minutes to lie down, tell yourself you are going to take a nap in order to reset your mind. Have the intention that, as soon as you wake, you will take back the reins of your thinking from a place of less velocity and less confusion. And when you wake, before getting up, spend a few moments cultivating gratitude for the good things in your life: your blessings, your breath, the fact that you have woken up at all and still have an opportunity to change your life. You may have a lot of work to do, but if all you accomplish in the minutes you are lying down is to remember that your life is supposed to feel good, to remember that you are here to learn how to take good care of yourself, it will have been a productive day.

253. ❧ THOUGHTS ARE TIME BOMBS

Worry less about thinking positively and more about thinking skillfully. "Positive" and "negative" are just two sides of the same coin, for when you know what you don't want, you are that much closer to knowing what you do. The trouble is that discontent is like dynamite: it can blow holes through obstacles or just blow you up, depending on how long you hold onto it. Time is the determining factor. The problem is not that you acknowledge your difficulties, but that you dwell so long with them. So today, when you find yourself complaining about something, imagine a fuse has been lit, a timer is ticking, and that you must make haste to direct the energy of your discontent into something that will actually serve you. Remember that it only takes a single moment to connect to your pain, a single moment to feel compassion for yourself, so you don't need to tell the story of your suffering in all its endless details. Learn to summarize: "I feel X because I need Y." Then move on to something that actually feels good: your breath, your blessings, the things that make you feel alive. Every cell in your body already understands your struggle, just as every coil in a compressed spring knows its own latent force. And so your job is not to dwell on your contraction, but to find enough joy to release resistance and let your life move into its natural expansion.

254. ∾ Not Every Branch Can Hold Your Weight

Discontent is a gift and a source of guidance. Not every branch on the tree of life can hold your weight, and the unrest you feel sometimes is just knowledge of that truth. Those who cannot live with their own discontent will never find stable footing, while those who blame their discontent on others will never learn to climb at all. So always remember: no one is in charge of this life, and though there are unseen forces that can sustain and support you, you will not find them till you attend to the restlessness inside you.

255. ∾ Kids Fighting in the Back Seat

How real are your dilemmas? When the heart is troubled, it's so easy to see life as a conflict between external choices, and to lose yourself in "Option A/Option B" thinking. It's good to remember that, most of the time, your options are like little kids fighting in the back seat of a car: their conflict is not really with each other, but with how long the journey is taking. And so, as parent to your own heart, you must turn to face your impatience, which is always your greatest problem, and remind yourself that struggling won't get you to where you want to go any faster. Today, notice the places in your life where you focus on conflict and contradiction, and remind yourself there of your wish to be happy—a wish that underlies and unites all the options you have ever considered or will ever consider. Say to yourself: "May I look after myself with ease." For soon enough, your time in this world will be done, and all the knots you've untangled or failed to untangle will matter far less than the joy with which your fingers have grasped the kite-string of your life.

256. ∾ GUILT IS A TEACHER

Try to learn something from your feelings of guilt. Most of us know on some level that guilt is not always productive, yet we still feel stuck with this feeling, no matter how we try to shake it off. Rarely do we see that guilt teaches us something: not that we are bad people, but that we are not yet getting what we need in order to be happy. We are so focused on the courtroom drama of whether or not we have failed others that we cannot see guilt for what it really is: a call to clarify our own needs and to understand that this life is spacious enough to accommodate many people's many different desires. For example, a man feels guilty that he doesn't want to spend his day off with his wife's parents. If he looks he may see that her need for family is perfectly compatible with his need for rest. A woman feels guilty that she dislikes her boyfriend's loud laugh. But if she looks she may see that his need for excitement is perfectly compatible with her need for peace. Your feelings of guilt are not accidental, not a detour on your way to otherwise feeling good. You have deliberately brought them into creation, for reasons it is now up to you to discover.

257. ∾ Volcano

Sometimes the best you can do is close your eyes and imagine you're screaming at the top of your lungs. You can learn a lot from that practice, actually. It teaches you to respect the volcano inside you. It also teaches you that you are not the volcano.

258. ∾ Resistance Means Progress

If you aren't meeting with resistance, you aren't trying hard enough. Whatever your path is, whatever you are trying to do with your life, the intensity of the resistance you face is always proportional to the strength of your effort. If you practice meditation, for example, you will see that the more you strive to be present, the more intensely restlessness, boredom, and self-doubt show up, just as the more money or fame you acquire, the more moochers and hangers-on come out of the woodwork. These difficulties are signs of your success, not your failure. In the same way, when people around you surprise you with their strong reactions to what you are doing, learn to interpret the charge you feel from them as a sign that your life is gathering momentum. And before you try to put out any fire, fix any problem, or prove anybody wrong, try to develop an attitude of appreciation for what stands in your way, just as a ballerina appreciates the hard earth beneath her feet and pushes joyfully against it in order to leap even higher. So today, notice the resistance within you and around you—uncooperative people, moments of self-loathing, plans that just won't come together— and try not sweep these aside with false self-confidence or the delusion that you are just experiencing bad luck. There is a lot to learn right here, and though there may be changes you need to adopt, remember: you are not lost. You are in the perfect position to make your next right move.

259. ∾ A Habit of Discouragement

You aren't always discouraged because the road is hard. Often, the road is hard because you get discouraged. For what is really asked of you in this life? To help others as best you can, to shelter them as best you can, to do your best to tend to the goodness inside you. None of this is beyond any of us, yet we stoop beneath the perception that some superhuman effort is needed to be happy, and we mistake the burden of our views for the weight of the sky. If things seem hard right now, you don't have to pretend they are easy. Just see that your discouragement is older than any of your troubles. Like a shadow, it has been following you a long, long time, but like a shadow, it will leave when you hold it to the light.

260. ∾ A Mood Is Not a Mountain

Don't let your mind sink into darkness. We often think of our moods as mountains we have to cross, no matter the distance or time it takes to travel them. But a mood is more like a compass showing you the direction you are facing. And just because you are facing south doesn't mean you have to keep heading south. And just because your mind is dark doesn't mean you have to follow that darkness to its end, hoping somehow you'll emerge on the other side. If you could only see that your task is not to solve all your problems at once, but rather to reorient yourself, to face in the right direction, you would start to have more faith in this journey you are on. So today, notice when your mind gets dark. Notice the small moments of self-loathing or comparison or simply the dull sense that you are somehow trapped by fate. And then use that information joyfully, as a navigator might delight to realize, "I see now! I got turned around." Just put your mind on your blessings, your breath, or anything that actually feels good to focus on. Don't worry about when you'll be arriving or how your pace compares to the pace of the guy next to you. One moment of discovering your true north is worth a thousand hours of walking in the wrong direction.

261. ∾ There Are Always Second Chances

There are always second chances. It may be true that every experience is unique and unrepeatable, but we are here for more than experiences. We are here for the happiness of the heart, a happiness that does not depend on getting this relationship or that opportunity, a happiness that always waits, because it is always there. Remember that the past can only reach you through the present, and so you always get the last move in this game of looking back over your life. If you find yourself regretting "the one that got away," remind yourself that all things slip away, and yet you still have this moment—a moment in which you can replace attachment with true love, self-pity with compassion, envy with appreciation, and worry with inner strength. Take your time; don't let anyone or anything rush you. Make your move only when you are moved from within.

262. ∾ Anxiety as Avoidance

Anxiety is often a form of avoidance. Worry can get into your system by presenting itself as urgent, yet a lot of the time, we face the future to keep from being present. Anxiety can cover over deeper loneliness and deeper sorrows that continue to nourish it from beneath the surface of awareness, like a system of roots. So if you really want to live with less fear and less worry, you are going to have to see that you are running—running from the fragile, unresolved present—and bring a spirit of honesty to what is happening right now. It's uncomfortable for you, like everyone else, to be here with all your uncertainties and insecurities. But if you bring your mind to your breath and try to make it as comfortable as you can, you will see that within the uncertainty of each moment and breath, there is also the possibility for great ease and strength. Like any task that you've been dreading, being present seems more difficult before you start doing it. So give it a try. The present moment is not just a place but a value, and the more often you value it, the more often you will find yourself taking refuge there.

263. ∾ Fixing a Hole Where the Rain Gets In

When you find yourself becoming fixated, try to see what is happening in terms of cause and effect. Strong desire and anxiety have a way of making you focus on how trapped and helpless you feel, and when these emotions are flooding your mind, like rain coming in through a hole in the roof, it's easy to forget that the real problem isn't that you are soaked and uncomfortable, but that you still haven't found the leak: the part of you that keeps letting these fixations in. So today, when you start to obsess about this or that, instead of trying to fix your fixations, like someone furiously mopping a floor onto which more water just keeps pouring, tell yourself: "Look, obsessions come and go, as storms come and go, but what's important right now is that I heal my mind." Healing your mind is not the epic task you might think it is. All you have to do, to heal, is meet your obsessions, one by one, with love and compassion. All the water that has fallen, the tears that have been cried, these will dry on their own. Let your vision be toward the future and your focus on not developing any bad habits while the storm is raging. If your obsessions ruin this day, and yet you do not let despair, self-doubt, or complaint take over your mind, it will have been a good day, when all is said and done.

264. ∾ Cheap Plastic Umbrellas

Worry is a cheap plastic umbrella sold in the middle of a rainstorm. It costs you so much and shelters you so little.

265. ❧ THAWING ICE

You are going to make some mistakes twice. You are going to make some mistakes hundreds of times. Get used to it. The vows you take to surround yourself with better people, to be kinder, to stop putting yourself in humiliating situations, cannot all be accomplished by a single stroke of the intellect, but only by developing a felt sense of how to be different in the same situations—just as you didn't learn to ride a bike by understanding how the gears work, but rather, by developing a "muscle memory" of what it's like not to fall even when you fear you will. That takes some time. If you pull food out of the freezer and try to eat it right away, you won't be able to. Only a fool thinks, "The food stays frozen, no matter what I do!" Anyone else can see that, in some small area, the ice is starting to thaw. So the next time you find yourself making the same mistake, look for the thawing parts: maybe this time around, you recover a little more quickly; maybe this time around, you are a little kinder to yourself. Resist the idea that these repetitions are exhausting. The only things that can exhaust you are your illusions—above all, the illusion that you were meant to get it right on the first try. When you truly understand that learning is the best that can be expected of any situation, you will find time and energy enough to become the person you always wanted to be.

266. ❧ BOREDOM

Boredom is a beautiful teacher. We say, "Oh, I'm too busy to be bored," as though a life filled with trivia were some great achievement. But boredom is actually a precious opportunity to see your life as it really is: a short plateau of days with a sudden drop at the end, an arrangement no amount of success or sex or fame or excitement can make satisfactory. You can let that information depress you, or you can see it as a call to start living your life, not by trying to squeeze the juice out of every experience as though it were an orange, but by slowly, gently letting the future separate from you, as whey separates from boiling milk, leaving you with only the purity of this unadorned moment. For what boredom is trying to show you, above all, is that every feeling is just a layer: when you get up in the morning dreading the eight hours of work ahead of you, that's just a layer; when you're at home on Saturday night not having all the fun you think you would be having if you were "out there," that's just a layer. And if you watch these layers instead of piling new layers on top of them, they start to peel back, revealing not only freedom but the confidence that you can, in fact, find happiness in your brief life. So today, when boredom comes, let it stay long enough to inspire you, to cause you to turn fresh eyes to the present moment. Distraction has its place too, but never let it push out boredom completely, for a life without some boredom is not a life, but a dried husk blowing in the wind.

267. ∾ You Are the Path

You are the path: it starts and ends with you. What else could be the meaning of all those bricks you have been carrying? All those resentments, sorrows, and distractions that keep you from doing your life's work—those are your life's work. And so you must embrace your burdens, not forever, but long enough to see how each is a piece of the road you are traveling. What frustrates you may not be fair, but it is showing you the frustration that is keeping you from being happy. So today, face your burdens with the following thought in mind: *No one is in charge.* No one is coming to turn your eyes to the light; no one is coming to show you the love you cannot feel on your own; no one is coming to make this world a place of peace. When you see that clearly, you will start practicing gratitude for what is, as though your life depended on it. For in fact, your life does depend on it.

268. ∾ IMAGINARY CRITICS

Don't waste your time defending yourself against invisible critics. People are much less aware of you than you think, preoccupied as they are with their own insecurities. More importantly, even when people do explicitly judge or condemn you, they are only ever expressing what is most alive in them: their own needs and feeling, all of which you share, believe it or not, though in different ways and at different times, by virtue of your participation in this common human experience. We all have a need for rebellion as well as for respectability, a need for self-expression as well as for privacy, a need for community as well as for aloneness—and so the criticism you are anticipating from others is usually just a sign that you do not yet believe there is room within you for your own different needs. So today, when you find yourself playing out a scene of conflict with someone else, remind yourself, "There's no one in charge here." That is, there is no one with the authority to place different needs into any sort of hierarchy. We're all figuring this out together, and the only categorical imperative is co-existence, which you will learn only by letting the diverse strands of yourself co-exist within you.

269. ∾ STEER BEFORE YOU PADDLE

Laziness is only very rarely the problem. Most people who seem lazy are really struggling with a lack of efficiency in their actions. If you turn a sailboat directly into the wind and tell yourself the only way forward is to paddle with your hands, you'll stop making effort pretty quickly. So when you feel you're not doing enough in some part of your life, it's important to remind yourself that your job is not to paddle but to steer. No matter how stuck things feel at work or in your relationships, your job is just to turn yourself in the right direction and forget about how far you manage to sail today. People are going to be angry with you sometimes; instead of trying to iron out every kink in every conversation, see if you can orient the whole relationship toward goodwill, knowing that today's tensions will be forgotten as soon as the relationship gains some forward motion. And if you feel you have done something wrong, apologize, but try to see your apology as pointing your compass toward a higher love, not as climbing a mountain or lifting a weight to atone for your sins. Just keep steering your life so that the wind is at your back. That in itself is a good day of work.

270. ∾ Expect Cooperation

Learn to expect cooperation as you move through life. We all have been betrayed by others, perhaps at moments when we needed their support most, but we have allowed these betrayals to blind us to the deeper forces of assistance and collaboration that are always present in every moment. Did you labor to create the cells and atoms that sustain your body every day? Did you invent the love that has nourished you for so many years? Everything you have is the result of cooperative components that you did not create by yourself. To harness this cooperative power of life, you must first incline your mind to it by developing thoughts of gratitude, for gratitude is how the heart gains access to invisible sources of helpfulness. Forget about what you are trying to accomplish for a moment. Focus instead on appreciating the things in your life that are trying to help: the friends who are thinking of you fondly, the breath that is trying to heal you as it moves through your body. Let it all in. You have to try, but you don't have to try alone.

271. ∾ The Web of Ordinary Courage

One of the greatest gifts we can give each other is the gift of fearlessness. It is a beautiful feature of this human life that we all are frightened by different things. As such, each of us is positioned to see beyond the mountain of someone else's anxiety, and through this web of ordinary courage, we can come to know how vast life is, how varied and filled with possibility its landscape. So today, if you want to do some good, find someone who is dreading something and sit with him or her a while. Sit, without letting pity or desire to give advice cloud your heart. Just be there with love, knowing that in your eyes, someone else is glimpsing new horizons.

272. ∾ TRAVELING COMPANIONS

Try to love your problems, for they are your truest traveling companions. So much of the violence in our world and in our hearts comes from the mistaken perception that our problems will destroy us if we don't get rid of them quickly. Someone does something you don't like, for example, and suddenly anger is there, riding on your back. But anger can only make you do something violent if you behave violently toward it first: by denying its right to exist, by trying to force it to be other than what it is. When you were a teenager and your parents did something embarrassing around your friends, you probably thought you'd die of humiliation. But you didn't die, and hopefully as an adult you have the wisdom to remind yourself, "What other people do is no reflection on me." So carry that wisdom into the way you regard your inner difficulties—your irritations, your sorrows, your loneliness, your deep sense of failure—none of which you asked for, none of which are reflections on who you really are. And if you can accept these uninvited visitors within you, you can actually start to put them to work. So today, whatever situations you find yourself in, whatever feelings are passing through you, try to develop an attitude of curiosity toward them. Ask yourself: "What good am I being asked to develop right now?". Within you there is a circus. Trust the members of that circus, and start to discover the talents each one possesses.

273. ❧ Setting a Broken Bone

Believe in your own ability to heal. When a bone breaks, a doctor can help with alignment, but it is ultimately the bone that does the healing, provided it has support and stillness. Your heart is no different. What feels broken in you will find wholeness in time if you can hold it with a quiet and steady mind. To do that, you must forget some of the thoughts and advice that are swirling around and within you, for they just put pressure on the pieces of your life that are trying to combine. Focus on your breath instead and think of it as a container in which healing can take place without resistance. As for the "truth" of the mistakes you think you've made, forget all that. Truth requires boundaries, and if you don't start setting some in your head, you'll never be able to trust anything, yourself least of all.

274. ❧ Looking Past

You have to learn to forgive yourself. Our culture is so anxious to teach us to forgive others, but just as you can't really love others till you love yourself, you can't really forgive others till you forgive yourself. Forgiving yourself is not a matter of apologizing. To forgive is neither to atone nor to condone, but rather to look past the desire and aversion that are clouding your mind to see the beauty that lies beyond them—just as, every morning, I look past the ugly buildings outside my window to glimpse the blue sky behind them. Forgiveness, in the end, is a matter of focus, a promise to yourself that, because you want to have a free heart, you will not allow your perspective to be narrowed or confined. So today, reflect on some of the ways you have hurt yourself in body, speech, and mind: neglect you have paid your physical being, words by which you have made your life less beautiful, cruel thoughts you have inflicted on yourself. Take some time to feel the pain in these and to feel your impulse to retaliate against yourself for what you have done. But then say to yourself instead, with as much sincerity as you can: "For all the ways I have hurt myself, knowingly or unknowingly, I still forgive myself." When you can mean these words with all your being, you won't have to struggle so hard to forgive others, for you will have seen the light in yourself, and you will know that light to be the same light that exists in them.

275. ∾ A Clean Shirt for a New Day

Regret has its positive uses. You can wear it as a chain, but you can also wear it as a clean shirt to honor a new day. The boy dressed up for his Friday night date doesn't feel his clothes as a weight or a fetter. He knows what we all should: that love means wanting to be better.

276. ∾ Nothing Fell Down the Well

We often think of letting go as dropping something precious down a well, and it is the thought of this deprivation that keeps us from moving on. So it's good to remember that letting go is just letting be: letting all things be what they are without sewing a thread of pain into their fabric. Whether what you love is four feet in front of you or four thousand miles away, the truth of our separation from each other always coexists with the eternal nature of love. These two follow us through life like light and shadow, and our task, like that of a painter, is to perceive both at once. So you don't have to pry your fingers loose from your dreams. Just love what you love and hold it in your heart even as your eyes release it.

277. ∾ We Will Meet Again

You don't have to fix the past, for you will certainly meet it again. The setting and characters may change, but the lessons you have yet to learn will be the same. And there, the real question will not be whether you have found a neat resolution to all your problems, but whether you have found a vantage point from which to see them clearly as they re-arise. This is the problem with regret, for just as a clock that runs five minutes too slow is less accurate than one that doesn't run at all, your habit of chewing over what just happened five minutes ago gives you less clarity than you would have if you just sat still and waited for the problem to come around again. So today, notice your tendency to replay situations in your head just after they occur. And then remind yourself that, moment by moment, you are shaping your life with your present intentions. If Moment One, Moment Two, or even Moment Five Billion have been failures, well here you are in Moment Five Billion and One: free to choose your thoughts. Just bring your awareness to your heart and try to feel the love and compassion that have always been there, unaffected by any of your errors. And when your mistakes find you, as they will, let them be like those high school bullies you meet again later in life who cannot hide their amazement at how admirably you've changed.

EQUANIMITY

(*winter*)

278. ~ When the Road Is Snowed Over

Take care of the moments in your life when everything seems to have come to a standstill, when the roads of your life are all snowed over and all your best-laid plans are broken. Guard against the impulse to force healing by falling back on strategies you've already tried or feelings you've felt many times before. Remind yourself that healing is not something you do, but rather a property of who you are. Your real work is to seek correct alignment, just as a doctor might actually break his patient's bone a second time in order to line it up correctly with the rest of the skeleton, knowing full well that healing happens on its own, in good time. In the same way, your work is not to create momentum out of thin air by making yourself more busy, but rather to bring yourself into the correct understanding that momentum is always there beneath the surface of your life, waiting to be tapped. So today, instead of struggling with your surroundings, bring your attention into your heart and try to feel the uncreated happiness that is always already there. And when you find you cannot feel, practice feeling numbness, and practice feeling the absence of connection to your heart. The sooner you learn to feel no-feeling, to stay present to what is still veiled to you, the sooner the wheels of your life will start turning again.

279. ~ When You Can't Create You Can Work

You must learn how to wait for the openings in your life, those moments when the truth of your pain and the path that leads away from it are revealed. Our problem is that we want every moment to be an opening. We want twenty-four-hour access to all of life, including our emotions and wisdom, and so we forget that not every moment can be a revelation. We forget that, in fact, our obsession with trying to form conclusions about our lives is a way of not actually living them. That doesn't mean you have to be passive. As Henry Miller once said, "When you can't create you can work," a statement that applies not just to art but to self-understanding. You cannot create clarity about your life, but you can work to develop the conditions in which clarity can show up. So today, notice where you are trying to force wisdom and look instead for the other good qualities you could be developing: your generosity, your good humor, your patience. Approach your heart as someone might approach a to-do list: happy to take care of the small stuff, item by item. There will be time for feeling great things—for learning big lessons. But for now, just make sure the floor of your workshop is well swept.

280. ∾ THERE ARE NO BREAKS

Don't keep waiting for a break. There are no breaks in the unbroken flow of time, and every moment, pleasant or unpleasant, is equally important in deciding your destiny. We have this unhelpful habit of dividing experience into "meaningful" and "meaningless" segments, trying to figure out how one area of life can relieve us of the burden of having to be present in other areas—as though an hour of yoga or meditation or exercise could prepare us, like mechanical clocks, for running mindlessly and efficiently through the rest of the day. But this is why we feel so ungrounded much of the time, for in fact, there is only one certain ground in this shaky life. And it is not a technique or a person or a religion, but rather the continuity of your wholehearted attention. So try to make this day "in the shape of a circle," as Ajaan Mun said. Remind yourself, as often as you can, that "this moment too is important," and honor that importance by putting your mind on your breath, your heart, and your many blessings. Awareness is your true ground. That other thing you are standing on is already starting to fall apart.

281. ∾ You'll Deal with That When It Comes

Faith is not so much a matter of trusting the unknown as refusing to distrust it. You don't have to believe that everything happens for a reason or that some beneficent force is watching over you. All you have to do is see how empty your distrust is, how it comes and goes for reasons that are mostly disconnected from the outside world, and how, at any moment, you really have only two choices: to think painful thoughts or not. So today, when anxieties arise, don't try to convince yourself that everything is going to be okay. Tell yourself instead: "I have the strength to meet whatever comes with an open heart." If your partner leaves you, you'll deal with that when it comes. If they fire you or evict you, you'll deal with that when it comes. If the love you sow comes up as regret, you'll deal with that when it comes. But only when it comes, for no sane soldier abandons his post to run out, empty-handed, across enemy lines. So stay where you are, sheltered by the thought that, step by step, you have what it takes to live step by step.

282. ∾ Time Expands in Proportion to Love

You have enough time. It is true that death can come at any moment, but the purpose of that reflection is to remind you to get started, today, on the work of your heart—not to worry about whether or when you will finish that work. Time expands proportionally to love, and so your task is just to put your hands in the clay and keep them there watchfully, trusting not only that something beautiful will come, but also that, however far you get, the distance will have been enough. If you are eighty when your heart finally opens, and all you catch is a glimpse of your true love crossing the street, that will have been enough. If you finally get past your inner critic and have only the strength to write a single word on a piece of paper, to paint a single brushstroke on a corner of canvas, that will have been enough. If at last you learn to live for yourself, not for the expectations of others, and you are left with just a single day to express that truth, that will have been enough. To live in alignment with the heart, not to justify it with works and results—that is the best that can be expected of a human being. So make that thought a temple into which you let no worry, worldly or spiritual, ever enter.

283. ∽ Today Is Better Than Yesterday
Today is better than yesterday, because today you still have the chance to meet your troubles with love.

284. ∽ We Are All in the Process of Being Forgotten
We are all in the process of being forgotten. It is how you hold this truth that determines your happiness. You can cling to thrones of straw, straining more and more each year to be seen as king or queen of this or that. You can resent the next generation, festering behind the mask of everything you think you have learned. Or you can get down to the work of understanding what it means that we all are one. For we all are one, not perhaps in body or mind or deed—but at heart, in the sense that there is no one "out there" whose success you cannot rejoice in as deeply as though it were it your own—because it is your own. When you start to see this, aging takes on a different tone. Look out the window: the birds are not singing

for you; the rain is not falling for you; this planet does not spin for you. And yet the joy you sense in every thing is yours.

285. ∽ Freedom Before Answers

The hardest decisions you will ever make will involve whether to walk away from things and people you love or to try a little harder. No one can answer these questions for you—and in all likelihood, neither can you right now. Most of life unfolds in the uncertain space between holding on and letting go. But what you can do is bring a sense of freedom to your difficulties, remembering that freedom is not something we are given only after we answer all the questions, but rather, something we are born with and can connect to even in the midst of uncertainty. We are free, above all, to choose our intentions. So ask yourself, "What would it be like to try a little harder out of love?" and search for the part of yourself that already knows how to do that. And then ask yourself, "What would it be like to walk away out of love?" and search for the part of yourself that already knows how to do that. You will know that you are free when you know that love is there either way. And the great irony is this: it is only when we see inwardly that we can be happy regardless of our external decisions that the right life-choices suddenly become clear.

286. ∽ The Traveler and Her Shadow

Be patient when your deeds don't match up to your wisdom, for action lags behind consciousness as a shadow behind a traveler. And yet wherever one goes, so must the other follow.

287. ∽ Disappointment

We are so frightened by disappointment. So many of our big emotions like anger or sorrow exist to hide the more subtle truth that we feel let down by our lives and are scared that disappointment will destroy us if we face it. Whole branches of pop-psychology exist to reassure us that other people are "pathologically" this or that, just so we don't have to admit that others aren't what we hoped they'd be. And within our own minds, too, whole complexes of self-judgment or defensiveness exist, just so we don't have to admit that many of our mental habits simply don't serve us. The Buddha called this slow, gradual process "disenchantment"—the clear seeing that a lot of how we think about life doesn't actually help—but "disappointment" is a good translation too, because just as we feel let down by others yet are frightened of admitting, "Wow, I thought I could depend on you, but I see now I can't," so too we are constantly disappointed by our own emotions and scared of admitting this. So it helps to remember that true love lies on the other side of disappointment. Until you have seen your own flaws or those of another, you haven't really loved. So today, when you find yourself lost in thought, ask yourself, "Is this thought serving me?" and be willing to face the disappointment that may arise if the answer is no. Your clear seeing will not kill you. When you can look at disappointment without flinching, you will learn its other name: wisdom.

288. ∾ THERE ARE NO QUALIFICATIONS FOR BEING HUMAN

There will come a time when what you are good at and what actually makes you happy diverge, and you will have to feel your way through the darkness to reach your heart's true destination. Try to remember that there are no qualifications for being a human being; unlike machines, which are made for specific purposes, we humans have no function. It is only the dishonest among us who tell us what we are meant to do in order to convince us that we should value their expertise over what we feel. And within you too, there are the same dishonest impulses, which urge you to do things simply because you can succeed at them: to work where praise or money is easy, to be sexual where attention comes quickly, to be spiritual where the illusion of purpose goes unquestioned. And so it is a good practice, whenever you find yourself succeeding at something, to ask, "But where does this path actually go?" For many experiences are "good" but lead nowhere, and others are "bad" but lead somewhere important, and you must come to think of yourself less as a train conductor of your life and more as a worker laying track. If you incline in the direction of what makes you happy, you will eventually develop the skills you need to travel that path, but the opposite is not true: you can spend a lifetime developing yourself without ever gaining a sense of the goal. So today, make a list of a few things you think you aren't good at but intuitively feel are important to who you want to become, and try to generate a sense of excitement just to be learning in these areas, to be in over your head with something wonderful. For though it may feel good to be someone you can admire, there is a greater prize: to become someone you can actually trust.

289. ∾ RESPONSIBLE FOR THE RAIN

We often feel we aren't responsible enough. The truth is, we feel responsible for far too much: this crumbling body and wild thicket of anxieties, none of which we ever asked to have, and none of which we need lay claim to now. Even our mistakes, so central to who we think we are, are just light from a long-dead star. So when chaos comes into your mind today, remember that your main duty is not to anything arising in any moment, but to whether you meet each moment with love. You are not beholden to the rain that falls where it may, but only to the thatching of your little hut.

290. ∽ CLARITY IN ITS OWN TIME

Clarity comes in its own time. Doubts settle eventually but unpre-dictably, like flakes of snow in a shaken snow globe, and the best thing you can do to speed up this process is just be still, lest your restless mind muddy the waters of your heart. Right now, there may be relationships or situations that are confusing you, and from this confusion, you may feel an urge to extract clarity or closure from what is still undefined. But look and see if your urge does not come from a deeper sense of scarcity, a sense that your time and options are running out, and remind yourself that wisdom, like love, is always abundant. You can let go of your conclusions, just as you can let go of those who love you, and trust that the right ones will still be there in the morning. If you feel you must do some-thing with your thoughts right now, then take out a sheet of paper and write a letter that you promise yourself you will never send. When you are finished, reread what you have written, feeling the pain and panic between the lines. And then, whatever else you end up doing, say a prayer of thanks for all the wrong words left unsaid, and for all the hasty messages left undelivered.

291. ∽ TUGGING ON A BALL OF STRING

We lose our hearts in the details. Life is hard sometimes, but when we hold this truth generally, we find that difficulty can coexist with great joy. The trouble comes when we pull at the details of a prob-lem prematurely, and, like a child tugging on a ball of string, just tighten the knots more. So whatever you are struggling with today, try to think about it more generally. You can think, *This is hard for me*, or *I'm stuck around this issue*, but above all, when the voices in your head come around and ask for specifics, think of that ball of string and remember that it is only when you hold a tangle with a loose grip and a patient mind that the true thread to unravel it will appear.

292. ∽ OUR SHARED FADING

We are not only separate from each other, we are separating. With every moment, every breath, we are outgrowing the points of connection that bind us. No matter how much you love someone, you will have to lose him or her many times in the course of one life, let alone following the breakup of the body. This truth terrifies us, but comprehending it is also our one chance at experiencing intimacy in this life. For the thinking mind, with its concepts of relationship and obligation, can never see others truly as the changing beings they are. But the heart knows that we are all disappearing, and in our shared fading, are closer to each other than the veins beneath our skin.

293. ∽ STINGINESS WITH TIME

Perhaps the greatest stinginess is not giving things enough time. Rather than asking what we can give, we come to most experiences already asking what we can get. We withhold patience from life, in fact, far more than we withhold money from friends. And so we forget: stinginess with time is the main reason we never feel we have enough of it. People often say, "If only I had more hours to do what makes me happy," not realizing that, in their narratives of frustration, time is a metaphor for a loss of control over this uncontrollable world. One of the things that happens when we start to give time to our work, relationships, and inner lives without constantly expecting results is that we find we have more time than we thought to grow—just as when we practice generosity with material resources, we find we are less poor than we imagined. You will never have enough time to hold on to this changing life, but you still have plenty of time to find the joy that comes from letting go.

294. ～ Fear of Making Mistakes

So many of our deepest fears come down to a simple fear of making mistakes. Fear of death is often just fear of not having accomplished enough in life. Fear of separation is often just fear of not having been successful enough at a relationship. And while there may be truth in these fears, truth that we have not yet learned to live as well as we might, we must always remember that life is not a first-grade classroom where everything depends on answering the teacher's question correctly. In a very real sense, you cannot get life right, nor can you get it wrong. But you can live well, if what you mean by that is not finding freedom from mistakes but freedom in making them. One way to do that is to look at the conflicts in your life as the engine of your inner growth. People are going to be upset with you sometimes. People are going to accuse you of all sorts of things. You can judge them resentfully or judge yourself guiltily—or you can face your fear of making mistakes once and for all. So when someone criticizes you, ask yourself: "If I am wrong, what possibilities of living does that open up for me? And if I am right, what possibilities of living does that open up for me?" Let every confrontation expand you, in other words, for indeed, that is the very purpose for which it has entered your life.

295. ～ How Long Do You Want to Be Involved?

Learn to judge your actions according to the amount of anxiety they bring. We often get hung up on ideas of right and wrong, are forever saying things like, "I told a little lie—does that make me a bad person?" But that's the wrong question. You have an innate goodness and are worthy of love, no matter what you do. And yet, the real danger in lying or cheating or lashing out is the amount of looking over your shoulder you will have to do afterwards. These actions inevitably bring anxiety, and over time, it is anxiety that will obscure your heart and disconnect you from your inner goodness. So today, before you act in any difficult situation, ask yourself: How long do I want to be involved with this? You may be "right" to lose your temper, but will the amount of time it takes to clear your system of anger and adrenaline be worth a single moment of feeling justified? And conversely, when people say you are "wrong" for living your truth and being who you are, will the amount of time you spend agonizing over their good opinion be worth a single moment of avoiding their blame? Ajaan Fuang once said that, to be happy, you have to think like a thief, and the first rule of thievery is always to have an escape. So praise yourself when you decide not to send that hostile email or engage in that worthless conversation. You just got away with two of the most valuable treasures known to humankind: free time and peace of mind.

296. ⚬ THE TRUEST SIGN OF FREEDOM

What is freedom? One good definition is that it is the opposite of addiction. Our culture teaches us to think of freedom as something resembling a beer commercial: beautiful people on a yacht, smiling at each other in approval. But this image reveals many of our deepest addictions—not just to alcohol, but to status, gain, praise, and pleasure. There's nothing wrong with a good party, of course, but as we get older, it's important to begin to measure our freedom not by images or ideas, but by the amount of clinging and craving in our minds. So go for a walk today, without any bags, plans, or destinations, and as you walk, reflect on any resistance you might have to the pure act of walking. Do you find yourself wanting headphones in your ears or beautiful sights in your eyes? Do you find yourself thinking about something else or wanting the act of walking to mean something profound? There are a thousand twists and turns of the mind that keep us from being free. Just ask yourself: "What would it be like to walk without wanting anything, to feel the way you may have felt, perhaps, in some foreign city where you were content to be no one at all, to be nothing but a smile in a sea of faces? For the truest sign of freedom is no sign of it at all?"

297. ∾ THIS UNRAVELING WORLD

The world is unraveling. Look closely at your new clothes: you will see a thousand threads already separating from the fabric. Look at your mind and you will see a thousand thoughts rebelling against the sense of self you've tried so hard to cultivate. And in the midst of this, it's easy to see love as one more unraveling thing, one more garment constantly wearing out. But love is not the material but the tailor; it is just as comfortable taking apart a suit in order to learn from it as weaving together a new one. So today, try to be the tailor. If things come together for you, you can develop joy; if they come apart, you can develop wisdom. You can always develop love. For life is too short to waste fighting this great unraveling, especially when all we have to do to be well is work skillfully with the cloth in our hands.

298. ∾ TAKE OFF YOUR SUNGLASSES

People are quick to believe they can control life, but slow to believe they can change their attitude to living it. They think they are free to turn up the brightness of the sky, but powerless to take off their sunglasses.

299. ∾ STRESS IS A PROPERTY OF THE WORLD

One of the biggest mistakes you can make is to try to get rid of your anxiety. We have so much shame about anxiety, and for so many of us, spiritual practice is a cosmetic tool for hiding our worries from sight. But in this way, we make our troubles worse, for the root of anxiety is trying to control what cannot be controlled, and until you look at your desire for control (rather than trying to control that desire) you will never be free from torment. As children, we were confronted with the instability of the adults in our lives, and we learned to think it was our fault when those adults let us down, for guilt gave us a sense of power over what was happening. And now as adults, we still unconsciously seek out anxiety in our jobs, relationships, and self-perceptions, for as long as we are anxious, we think, there is something we can fix. None of this brings any lasting peace, The real work of growing up is to make a shift from focusing on stress to focusing on the stressful nature of things. As Ajaan Chah said, when a glass of water breaks, we must learn to understand that it didn't break because someone wasn't careful enough, it broke because it is in the nature of glass to break. So today, try to apply this perception to your life. When you find yourself getting worried about work or love or money, remind yourself: "Stress is a property of the world, not something I'm doing wrong." Don't think that, by looking at life this way, you are being careless. Just the opposite: the more you can let life be inconstant, the more passionately you can love and care for it as it actually is.

300. ∾ THE INNER CHORUS

Everything we say to others out loud returns as a voice in our own minds. So much of the inner chorus of critics, babblers, and fools that daily deafen our heads and derail our dreams has been picked up from the same words we have dropped from our own lips. If we understood this, we would take the same care in choosing our speech as we do in choosing our life companions, for in many ways the two are one and the same.

301. ∾ TRY TO SEE THE JOKE IN IT

If you want to live in the present moment more, learn to laugh at yourself. We tend to have a very narrow and somewhat cruel sense of comedy, and so we forget that one of the larger, evolutionary functions of humor is to alert us to our mistakes in a way that doesn't threaten our equilibrium. When we try to be present in a humorless way, it usually only takes a few moments of distraction to derail our efforts completely. But if you can see how funny it is that, with all the bounty and goodness of life before us, we nevertheless choose to think such painful thoughts, your mind will be more inclined to settle down right here in the present. Thanissaro Bhikkhu likes to remind his students of a Far Side cartoon in which a cow in a field looks up and says, "Grass! We've been eating grass all these years!" It is in those moments when we see that what we thought was normal is in fact very strange that we truly start to grow. So today, when you find your mind wandering into thoughts of the past or future, try to see the joke in what is happening. You can take all the classes and read all the books, but in the end, it will be laughter that gets wisdom under your skin.

302. ∾ LIGHT FROM A LONG-DEAD STAR

Try to see the world around you in the past tense, for that is mainly where it exists. The trees, sprung from seeds long ago, are mostly just playing out their pasts. The people, born from wombs long ago, are mostly just playing out their pasts. And even our thoughts, which we try so desperately to control, are mostly just the consequence of thoughts thought long ago—they, too, are relics of a distant past. What is truly alive in the present moment is the choice about whether to relate to all this history with love and appreciation or else with resentment. What has history taught us? Not much, judging by our perpetual wars. But we forget that war is not an accident, but the result of our failure to let what is past be past. It is a failure we repeat not just on the grand scale of politics but every day, in the way we refuse to embrace our own contradictions. Both around and within us, we are constantly trying to annihilate parts of our lives and parts of ourselves we don't like, never realizing that these parts are like light from long-dead stars: they are already gone and not our legacy, though the frustration and anger we create around them will be. So today, look at your life as an historian would. Try to appreciate the conflicts within yourself as inevitable parts of a larger story. Try to learn from them. You cannot stop a war that has already happened, but there still is time to find some peace.

303. ∾ KEEP YOUR HANDS IN THE CLAY

Try not to confuse goals with deadlines. Our habit of only working on the parts of life that can be done to a clock is one of the ways we die before we're dead. This doesn't mean we shouldn't have goals, but that we should think of them as reasons for living rather than tasks to complete. For every outer accomplishment is only worthwhile according to some inner virtue such as patience, persistence, wisdom, or appreciation, and these are qualities we can start cultivating today. So wherever you are, put your hands in the clay and keep them there. As for when your work is done, that has nothing to do with you or your contentment.

304. ∾ ROOTS HIDDEN IN THE EARTH

Don't be afraid to keep some secrets. Your strength, like that of an oak tree, relies on roots hidden deep below ground. There may be part of you that is ready to flower and be appreciated, but there are other parts that will wither if brought to light too soon. Remember that it is more important to feel the fullness of who you are than to reveal that fullness to everyone all the time. Keep your practice to yourself. So as you give yourself to others today, hold back a part of your awareness and keep it planted in your body. Strange as it may seem, this withheld part is the key to deeper intimacy with the world and those around you. For others, too, have their secret roots, and as you come to dwell in your own mystery, they will sense in you not aloofness but aliveness, and you in turn will feel that much less misunderstood.

305. ∾ It's Not Like You Live Forever
One of the many reasons to reflect on the truth of death is that it can help you deal with all your little fears about aging and illness that arise in the course of a day. When this pain or that symptom comes, our medical ruminations mostly make us more anxious and incapable of facing the unknown. But if you can remind yourself, "Look, it's not like I'm going to live forever," you will find a sense of comfort and freedom from having to feel or be other than you are. In reflecting on death, you will also come to know this related truth: that you still do have a little more time, whether that time is twenty more years or just this breath. But you do have time—time to look into your body, not as you fear it to be, but as you occupy it from within. Look. If you have a breath, you still have strength somewhere. You have, at least, this very moment to lift your mind above anxiety and into a place of undying love.

306. ∾ Opportunity Costs
There is a cost to every opportunity. Every hour you spend on self-promotion is an hour you aren't spending on self-development. Every hour you spend complaining about a problem is an hour you aren't working on its solution. Our advertising culture tells us that we can come to a fork in every road and take both paths, but every moment we give consideration to advertising is a moment we aren't

considering the truth. The truth is, we have to learn to take joy in opportunity costs, to understand that when we aren't somewhere else—on an Instagram-filtered beach or in the arms of some passing pleasure—we are inevitably, thankfully, right here: the only place from which we can ever change our lives. So today, when you find yourself focusing on all the things you want but don't yet have, make a list of all the things you could joyfully, truthfully do without. Do you really need that last piece of food? Do you really need the last word? Do you need to pick up your phone? If letting go of something feels like deprivation, don't try to let go of it yet. But do try to make a game, as you go through this day, of counting all the numerous, passing desires that you could honestly pass by without causing yourself any sorrow. If you can build momentum in renouncing what is small, you will find it easier and easier to attain what is great.

307. ～ No Goodness but in Peace

Let your decisions be once you have made them. Perhaps they were good, perhaps not. But there is no goodness except in peace, and no way to know the value of a choice till you can settle down with it. Remember that everything you hope will make you happy in this life is just a reflection of your heart's deeper wish to be still, to stay with one thing and not have to leave or lose it. So accept whatever it is you have done and live its consequences fully. It is not the ending of a story, but the premise of a new one you now must embrace.

308. ～ Keep on Driving

The hardest thing in life is to keep a straight course. We love to turn—from this belief to that one, from this relationship to that one, from this practice or schedule to that one. And there may be some real changes you need to make, but most change is a matter of sticking with things long enough to see them actually change, just as a man heading north toward a city in the north will only see the truth of his direction by continuing to drive, not by looking out the window and wondering why he isn't yet where he wants to be. You have within you this constant compass: the compass of appreciation. Wherever you can appreciate your life as it is right now, wherever you can find perfect alignment with the person you want to be even in the midst of all your imperfections, wherever you can separate external appearances from your inner orientation to love and compassion—there is your true north. So don't mistake your impatience for a need to be saved. You're doing fine on your own. You just need to keep driving.

309. ∾ In Your Heart Is a Kitchen

If you look to a day to bring you a certain experience, you are bound to meet with disappointment. But if you think of a day as an opening in which to cultivate your goodness, no amount of difficulty can keep you from finding a satisfaction that runs deeper than any experience. In your heart is a kitchen; stay there, and prepare the patience, goodwill, and serenity that sustain you and those around you. For outside, in the company of expectations, the conversation is tense and exhausting. But inside, in this place of pure giving, your work is already your rest.

310. ∾ Your Belting Voice

So much of inner strength comes from learning to be vulnerable. Vulnerability is not, as we often think, an explosion of emotion, like hitting a piñata so our worst impulses can spill out everywhere. A lot of vulnerability has to do with recognizing our judgments of others, for our judgments of others are one of the main ways we defend against our own deeper feelings. So today, see if you can risk having wants and needs without pinning the blame for them on those around you. Understand that you are giving up your need to be right in exchange for fulfilling your need to be strong, for as soon as you are alone with what your heart truly desires, your whole being will begin to fortify and protect it. A vocal teacher told me once: We do not hurt our voices by screaming, but only by holding back a part of ourselves. And it is the same with your deepest cries of sorrows, which in their purity contain only peace.

311. ∾ KNOW WHEN YOU'VE MADE YOUR POINT

One of the greatest skills in life is to know when you've made your point. In life, as in art, nearly everything we do or say after we make a point detracts from that point. If you continue to berate people once they understand their mistakes, the truth of your criticism becomes tinged with pettiness and anger, like a dish that keeps burning even after it's taken off the stove. If you keep looking for reactions to your affection, your love becomes mixed up with attachment and possession. The worst of it is that, as you treat others, so you condition your own mind: not being able to drop an external conversation leads to not being able to drop an internal obsession. So today, for your own sake as well as others', try to develop sensitivity about the precise moment when you get your message across. No one likes to be lectured, your own mind least of all. Do you think you should be working harder, losing weight, succeeding faster? You probably already hear that voice loud and clear. Try having some compassion for the parts of yourself you've been yelling at, and they might be in a better mood to pitch in and help get something done.

312. ∾ DIGGING FOR DOUBT

If you want to live more fearlessly, you have to dig to expose the roots of your self-doubt. People often say, "I used to doubt myself, but I don't anymore." That sort of fake self-confidence might make for a good Facebook meme, but it won't make you happy. In Buddhist tradition, the abandonment of self-doubt occurs only at the first stage of total enlightenment. So unless you think you're there, you might want to explore some places in your life where you still doubt yourself. Do you doubt that you are worthy of love even if you lack a good career or a good relationship? Do you doubt that you can be happy in spite of the sickness, old age, separation, and death that you will inevitably meet with? Do you ever feel that you work hard and yet still are unmotivated when it comes to doing the things you really want to be doing? If you answered yes to any of these, there's still work to be done. The best way to deal with self-doubt is not to prepare a court case against it, but rather to ask yourself: "How do I know this self-doubt is true? Has a team of scientists independently verified my fears?" If you look, you will see that self-doubt is usually the least scientific thing in the world, and you will find it tends to evaporate quickly when brought into the light of consciousness.

313. ∾ IRREVERSIBILITY

At any moment, you really only have two jobs: to be kind and to be honest. You may think that life requires more meddling than this, so it's good to remind yourself that there is a part of life that goes somewhere, and a part that just goes in circles. Your task is to take care of the first and let the second take care of itself. If you try to clean your house in such a way that dirt will never accumulate again, you will only drive yourself crazy. And yet, we often approach love in this same way and try to make others feel and act toward us in a way that is not subject to reversal. But the girl in the coffee shop who just smiled at you has already turned her gaze away, and the admirer who used to call or bring flowers has forgotten to today—and in all this, we fail to see that the real sadness is our insistence that we take on a job we were never equipped to perform: to make the world in our own image. And so you must learn to delegate, not just to your fellow workers, but to life itself. Let pleasure and pain take care of themselves. Let gain and loss take care of themselves. Let praise and blame take care of themselves. If you pour into kindness and honesty the same energy you pour into these changeable things, you will find a happiness that is irreversible.

314. ∾ GROWTH AND FREEDOM

Don't confuse balance with inertia. Ajaan Maha Boowa said that, for most people, the Middle Way is "the middle of the pillow." True balance comes from a willingness to make new decisions, new mistakes, and new adjustments in response to feedback from your life. Like a tightrope walker who leans to the left and then to the right, a balanced life does not stand still but teeters back and forth constantly between growth and freedom, between pushing for progress and then resting content with life as it is. So ask yourself today: "Which do I need more of right now, growth or freedom?" Our culture teaches us that growth is always the answer, but is that true right now? Are you scared of committing to something important or are you fixated on making one thing work? The answer will be different on different days. Either way, you can help bring yourself into equilibrium by focusing on your breath. Sometimes we have to change our breathing to change our lives. Sometimes we just have to watch the breath, just as we have to watch life float past. But wherever we develop sensitivity about what feels good, we are slowly, surely coming into balance.

315. ∾ ECHO CHAMBERS

Try not to be afraid of your own irritation when it comes. Remember that your conscious mind, like a social-media site, is basically an echo chamber where like-minded voices congregate, giving you a false picture of what's really going on. When irritation, like a party crasher, comes, we often react impulsively by reasserting our ideals: "I should be nice," "I should be calm," etc. But there is more to your mind than your ideals, just as there is more to politics than what your friends think, and you must never shrink from any of the information that life brings you in the form of these uninvited emotional states. You can't control the arising of thought, but you can control what you do with your thinking. So today, when you suddenly find yourself getting irritated, try to meet that irritation with a spirit of discovery. A lot of times we are afraid of our own irritation because we believe others will not love us if we aren't easy to be around, so remind yourself that what people fall in love with is your love, not your perfection, and try to bring love to your own bad temper. The one you have been trying to exile holds the secret of your greatest growth. Make a place for it at your table.

316. ∾ TEENAGE MIND
People often say, "I wish I could control my thoughts." But you can't control your thoughts, you can only control your relationship to them. The mind is essentially a teenager; if you try to restrain it, you can be sure it's going to slip out a window at four in the morning to meet God knows whom. You'll get much further by acknowledging the mind's autonomy: it is free to think whatever it wants, just as you are free to live apart from its influence.

317. ∾ YOU DON'T HAVE TO CUT DOWN EVERY TREE TO MAKE A PATH THROUGH THE FOREST
It's not true that anything worth doing is worth doing well. There are plenty of things worth doing badly: awkward first drafts you just have to finish, difficult conversations you have to muddle through. Our educational system teaches us to think of every task

as a test, because people are more pliable when they think they are being tested, but if you look back over your life, it should be clear that very few tasks have actually changed the course of your destiny. Your poor performance on that sixth-grade history presentation didn't end up mattering all that much. The questionable color-scheme at your wedding didn't end up mattering. What did matter, if you really think about it, were the qualities of mind you developed in response to your challenges. All that anxiety and self-criticism you built up in high school? They're probably still with you today. Think of all the things you have been afraid to do with your life because you needed to do everything well. That's a sobering thought. And yet, it's not too late to develop the one skill that really does matter: the ability to remember the love you have for yourself at every moment, in everything you do. That love that is the real reason you do anything at all. If you could develop that kind of memory, you would see that there are an infinite number of ways to cut a path through the forest of your life. You would also see that you don't need to cut down every tree in order to make that path. So today, when things get tough for you, remind yourself: "This is not a test. This is an opportunity to remember what is important." Don't let your work make you forgetful, like the ambassador in Rumi's story who learns everything about the country to which he is sent, but forgets to deliver his master's message. Your happiness is the message you have been sent to deliver.

318. ❧ INNER SOVEREIGNTY

Inner peace is not inner standstill, so stop fighting the constant movement of your life. Inner peace is really an ever-changing, ever-loving conversation between parts of yourself. As such, it is closely related to the conversations you tend to have with people around you.

Take a look at these. Do you tend toward a lot of idle chatter? Or do you tend toward resentful silence, begrudging those who try to engage you? These outer habits are an accurate mirror of your inner being. So today, with everyone you meet, try to act like a king or queen among advisors: listen to everyone who crosses your path, not because everyone is to be automatically trusted, but because everyone might be carrying some piece of wisdom or information you need in order to rule over yourself. As you engage in external conversation more deliberately, you will find that your state of mind starts to change from dullness, on the one hand, or anxiety, on the other, to true tranquility. You will find yourself less at war with your thoughts and more at peace with who you are when you are not chasing after prizes or confrontations. And that kind of sovereignty is worth more than any power that exists between heaven and earth.

319. ∾ DANCING WITH CHAOS

Growth takes place in chaos. The more you need your life to follow a pattern, the more you need your latte made the same way each morning, the more you are no longer a human but a thing, incapable of growth or gratitude. We forget this, which is why we have to be specific when we find yourselves in chaos—public transportation that breaks down, emails that get no responses—about exactly what it is that you are learning right now. In the midst of all this upheaval, are you not developing patience, determination, equanimity, and good humor? And are these not the same qualities you need to accomplish your dreams and find happiness in this life? So today, try to dance with chaos rather than fight it. Follow it as someone learning to dance must follow a more experienced partner, turning this way and that, even though it may feel arbitrary or wrong at first. Follow it in all its disjointedness and confusion, trusting that you are learning something, and that your next right move is about to be revealed.

320. ∾ LIFE GOES SOMEWHERE

If you are learning something, you are moving forward. We resist the idea that life is a path that actually goes somewhere, mostly because we identify so closely with the pleasure, status, and material gain we encounter along the way—all of which, in fact, do go nowhere. But we are not our pleasure, our status, or our gain, and when we begin to see that these things are so impermanent—they cannot even be carried from one moment to the next—you begin to realize that what you truly carry with you in this life is what you have learned. Today, for example, you might feel anxious or depressed or even somewhat dead inside, and you might be tempted to conclude that none of the work on yourself you have done so far has accomplished anything, but that is because you are identifying with what is passing rather than with the lessons you have learned about what is passing. For the truth is that things are different this time around: you are stronger, your tools sharper, and your sense of humor is better. So try to pay more attention to the wisdom you have gathered and less attention to whether today is as pleasant as yesterday. If your memory and forgetting can work together in this way, you will be all right, no matter what comes at you.

321. ∾ WAIT FOR IT

Don't strain yourself searching for the lessons in your life: some may not be there yet.

322. ∾ THIS IS NOT A TEST

Life is not a test. We know this intellectually, but do we live that way? Would we stay so long with joyless jobs, relationships, and compulsions if we didn't feel pressure to prove we could be "good" at these things? Would we waste so much time immersed in trivia if we weren't running away from some perceived exam, like a kid who cuts class not because he doesn't want to learn, but because he is afraid he will fail at learning? If we truly understood that life is not a test—not a trial to prove our goodness nor an ordeal to win anyone's love—we would see each moment both as no big deal and as precious beyond all measure, an opportunity we can neither afford to force nor afford to waste. So today, look at the ways you live your life as a test, and start to imagine what it would be like to live in the absence of that perception. You have right here the greatest teacher there is: your breath. Just pose the question, "What kind of breathing would feel good right now?" and see how your body wants to respond. Remind yourself that there is no way in which you are supposed to breathe; there are no prizes to be won. There is only this short life in which to find the joy and peace that are your truest accomplishments.

323. ∾ One More Dream from Which to Wake
Fame is the illusion that life has a center. But life has no center; no one is famous to everyone, everyone is famous to someone, and each sense of rank we acquire as we go through life is just one more dream from which we will have to wake.

324. ∾ In Praise of Incompletion
There is incompletion at the heart of everything. Books don't really get finished, they just get sent off to the publisher. Relationships don't really get finished, the people in them just change and grow different. Life doesn't really get finished, it just transitions into what we cannot yet understand. As creator, not just consumer, of your experience, you will always create more worlds than you could

possibly inhabit. There is no failure or lack of responsibility in this, for the best that can be expected of you, a finite being, is that you bring your whole heart to the life you are weaving, a life whose pattern is unfolding faster than your ability to tie up loose ends. Learn to make lists of things you'll probably never do. The happiest and most creative people I know are list-makers, and over the years I've tried to follow their example. I keep lists of titles of songs I may never write, lists of books I may never read, lists of thoughts I may never fully articulate. Make lists of whatever thrills you, but above all, guard against making too many to-do lists, for nothing is more toxic than the notion that value comes from completing what by nature cannot be completed. If you practice making lists that are open-ended, you will find something paradoxical start to happen: the more you get excited about what you cannot fully master, the more mastery and progress you will make with it. When you learn to love the infinite longing within you, you can break off a little piece of it, and find that is enough to sustain you.

325. ∾ LIFE IS MEANINGLESS

Life is utterly meaningless. Everything you have will be taken from you. Everything you become will be undone by death. The irony is that the sooner you accept this, the sooner you can have gratitude for your life as it actually is. For what keeps us from being grateful is that we confuse gratitude with privilege: we think there are inherently meaningful objects in the world—possessions, relationships, and careers. When we have too much of these things, we fall into guilt, and when we have too little, we fall into resentment. If you get a break, someone will say, "You're lucky to have that." But you aren't lucky to have that: the more money you acquire, the more money you will lose some day; the more power you obtain, the more power you will have to part with. It is only when you realize that gratitude is not a response to privilege but an activity you engage in out of sheer will that you begin to see the freedom and possibility in life. So when the fear strikes you, and you think, *But what if I lose this?*, remind yourself that, yes, you will lose this. And yet, until you do, you have an opportunity to search for what cannot be lost. For in everything that dies, there is still the reflection of what is eternal, and as you pass through the mirror of gratitude, you will find things stay the same and yet are reversed, so that you can say with all confidence: life is utterly meaningful.

326. ∾ ONE DAMN THING AFTER ANOTHER

Life can feel sometimes like one damn thing after another—because life *is* one damn thing after another, a fact that has absolutely no bearing on whether you are happy or miserable. Life was one damn thing after another when you were a child playing football in the rain, or when you were a teenager staying up all night, struggling to express yourself in music or conversation or love. You didn't resent your exertions back then, for the world seemed abundant and big to you, and you were excited just to be allowed in the game. As you got older, the thought of perfection started to creep into things, and attending the class of experience became less important than getting the highest grade. But it's not too late to change. Go out walking in the nasty December rain. The grocery list of your life will not be completed. But if you pick a few items and give them your heart, the world will open all its secrets to you.

327. ∾ A KNOTTED BALL OF STRING

So much of pain comes from impatience. Your life may be a tangled ball of string, but nothing wounds you as deeply as your insistence that the first thread you pull at be the one that unravels the whole mess. It is so hard for us to grasp that we are deluded about what makes us happy and also fully capable of moving forward in spite of those delusions. It is hard for us to grasp that all learning is learning as we go. Be careful, therefore, about listening to other people's advice, for most of it is just rooted in impatience and a desire to solve all problems once and for all so we can get on with the business of living. Well, life doesn't work that way. You are going to have to make the same mistakes many times before you find the thread that lies beneath them all. So try to take some joy in tending to your knotted ball of string, or at least some patience. You're going to be working at this life a long time and it gets better every step of the way.

328. ∾ 1950S SCI-FI MOVIES

You have no idea what is going to happen next. All your speculations and worries about the future will very soon seem as silly as those sci-fi movies from the fifties that predicted we'd all be flying around in saucers by now. Whatever you think tomorrow will be, it will be otherwise. But if you really want to see the future, look at the state of mind you bring to today's disappointments. That is your future. For though we live in a field of possibilities too vast and varied to comprehend, the only seeds that ever sprout in that field are those we water with our awareness. That means that when you struggle against what you don't want, you are growing resentment and discontent, which will be your most certain inheritance tomorrow. So today, try to catch yourself when you are lost in worries about what is to come. Bring yourself back to the present with this thought: *I will arrive there soon enough. But who will I be when I arrive?* For though life is uncontrollable and unpredictable, it is not exactly like running across a minefield, but more like digging a trench from which you can meet your difficulties from a place of strength and leverage. So with love and with gratitude, make a trench that stretches across all of your awareness, and you will be okay, no matter what comes.

329. ∾ Jigsaw Puzzle Pieces

Learn to see your life as a puzzle. In any puzzle, you can't understand the parts without understanding the whole, and vice versa. And yet, we get so easily discouraged when the people in our lives only give us part of what we are looking for. Like frustrated children who can't yet see why a particular jigsaw piece won't fit into every other piece, we push our part(ner)s to fit into everything we experience, which is to say, to be perfectly shapeless and undefined, rather than appreciating their edges and contours—all because we can't yet see the larger pattern of our lives. If we could understand that everyone we meet is bringing us some quality or insight into the larger perfection we are creating together, we would neither cling so tightly to the ones we like nor push so strenuously against the ones we don't. So when you find yourself getting frustrated by difference, conflict, separation, or even death, remind yourself: "I feel upset because I don't know where this piece goes yet." Sometimes the best you can do is throw the pieces on the floor and stare at them for a while. But the sooner you develop the confidence that they all fit together somehow, the sooner you leave your habit of blaming a single part for not being the whole, the sooner the solution will jump out at you and seize you in its grasp.

330. ∾ A Spider at the Center of a Web

The waiting may be the hardest part, but it's also the most important part, for it is how we wait that determines our lives, our minds, and above all, our sense of timing. We often feel at the mercy of the world's pace and schedule, and it is out of this sense of powerlessness that we fill up the empty hours with chatter or cheap pleasures. But in reality, our experience of time has little to do with the world and everything to do with our ability to focus: when we put our minds on what actually feels good, we always find ourselves at the right place at the right time, like spiders resting content at the center of their webs. So today, when you find yourself waiting on some person or opportunity, remind yourself that this is precious time to practice—unhurried, uncomplicated time in which to train your mind to focus on what is good: your breath, your blessings, your heart. Soon enough, the wheels of your life will start to turn quickly and there will be little for you to do other than show up to your destiny. But for now, in the empty spaces, your power is still up for grabs. Seize it.

331. ∿ A Truckload of Shit

People want a method for transforming their lives because they're scared of wasting time and effort. But if you've seen a farmer use a truckload of shit to fertilize a single tree, you've seen the only method of transformation that works: Accept your waste, gather it together, and seek the higher purpose it serves.

332. ∿ A Hundred Bucks and Some Ingenuity

Low self-esteem doesn't come from a lack of success or a lack of evidence that you are good enough. Low self-esteem comes from a lack of skill in seeing that your happiness depends on your actions. I once met a stockbroker who told me that the most alive he ever felt was when he only had a hundred dollars and the conviction that he could turn that sum into a fortune through his own ingenuity. After he made his fortune, life actually got harder for him. Your self-esteem is no different. It doesn't matter how little you have to work with today, what kind of a mood you are in, whether things are working out for you, or whether you are practicing this or that self-improvement technique satisfactorily. It matters only that you start to see, in some small way, that when you invest your mind in the right thoughts, you start to feel a little better. The antidote to low self-esteem is experimentation. Make conscious lists, on paper or in your head, of new thoughts you want to try thinking, new words you want to try saying to yourself, new perceptions you want to try applying to your life. Try anything, but like a scientist, test everything and observe what results it brings. Above all, let go of the idea that you have to feel great all the time. There is no meaningful standard the heart can be held to other than freedom. All you have to do, wherever you are, is reach for the feeling of a little more ease, a little more momentum, and a little more relief to know that you don't have to cross an ocean, you only have to learn to sail with the wind at your back.

333. ∾ QUESTION YOUR WORK, QUESTION YOUR PLAY

Question your work and question your play. How much do you really need to work? We think it is only the necessities of life that force us to sweat and slave, but as my teacher used to say, when you consider that most money is spent on things that promote greed, hatred, and delusion, it becomes clear that, most of the time, we hurt ourselves working in order to hurt ourselves at rest. And how are you spending your playtime? Real play comes from embracing and learning from the strangeness of life, yet we spend so much time trying to squeeze satisfaction out of the same old patterns of consumption, trying to find leisure, as Marx said, in what for any other animal would be work: digesting huge quantities of food, chasing after sexual partners, overstimulating ourselves in the hopes of feeling more alive. We have forgotten the simple pleasure of having a body, of walking down the street on a summer day, of listening to the wind through the leaves. And yet, we have what it takes to remember our deep and innate capacity for ease. So today, start to question your work and play, not by subscribing to anyone else's life plan, but by paying attention to your own breath. Try to breathe in a way that feels good. If your grip on the breath gets too loose and your mind wanders, find creative ways of coming back, of taking an interest in what is happening. That is your work. If your grip on the breath gets too tight and your mind becomes tense, allow yourself to receive the breath and be nourished by it. That is your play. When you find a balance between doing and receiving, when you see that most of what you need to learn about work and play is right here at the tip of your nose, you will harm yourself less and less, more and more of the time.

334. ⟶ No Such Thing as a Private Resentment

There is no such thing as a private resentment. Everything we think or feel irreversibly alters the world in which we live. Your childlike aversions are the heirs to your future: teach them well, while they still look up to your example.

335. ⟶ The World Is a Canoe

You will never know how hard the others around you are trying. When a group of people carry a canoe together on their shoulders, each one secretly believes she is lifting more than her fair share of the weight. That is human nature, it seems. But in reality, all a person can ever know at any given moment is whether he himself is doing his best, or less than that. This world, too, is like a canoe, which we are all in danger of letting slip, thanks to our habit of blaming and believing that there is a judge who could weigh and measure our individual efforts. The salvation of this world, therefore, begins with this realization: there is no one in charge. You must live this truth, beginning right where you are, by realizing how useless it is to try to change someone else's mind without changing your own first. So today, when you find yourself thinking that others are not doing enough, remind yourself, "My happiness depends on my own actions," and look to see if you can't give a little more to the present moment. You may well be giving more physical energy than others are, but there is another kind of strength you still need to develop: strength of mind. For the greatest and most important strength is not found in pushing against the way things are, but in learning to recognize your thoughts of irritation and keeping yourself from identifying with them. That is the kind of strength that will change your life.

336. ∽ TAKING CRITICISM

Learn how to take criticism, for in that way lies your greatest growth. But remember, first, that taking criticism is not the same as agreeing with it. You are free, and under no obligation to submit to anyone's views or opinions. These are simply resources, provisions for you to choose from as you prepare for the road ahead. The diversity of beliefs in this world is no different than the diversity of restaurants in a city, none of which you have to eat at, or the diversity of languages on this planet, none of which you have to speak. They are there for the taking, if and when they serve your expansion. So when someone criticizes you, before you agree or disagree, take some time to run your attention carefully over her words, as a carpenter might run his hand over a piece of wood to test its smoothness or roughness. Trust yourself. If words like "selfish" or "lazy" feel bad to you, that's because they are—at least, bad for you right now—and you don't have to carry them with you. But underneath the judgments we are all so quick to react to, look and see if some jewel isn't lying hidden, some key that unlocks the secrets of this day, some message telling you what your next right move should be.

337. ∽ BRING THIS DAY TO COMPLETION

See this day through till its end. Bring it to completion, not by staying longer at the office or working harder, but by looking back on the hours that have passed with an eye to acknowledging what has worked. What good qualities have you cultivated today? Have you not developed, in some corner of your life, a bit more patience, kindness, or determination? Be specific about the parts of your life that are unfolding smoothly. And just as important, be general about what isn't working. Instead of cataloging your problems in detail, reach for a general sense of relief that this day will be over before you know it and you will have done what had to be done. At the end of a long stretch of hours, you don't have to do more than lie down and reflect on what a blessing it is just to rest. Do this not out of a sense that you have failed in other parts of your life, but out of a sense that, even as you lie there, you are reframing your experience, just as a master musician reframes the wrong notes her band plays and turns these into some unexpected harmony. If you can go to bed each night with this sense of relief in mind, you will wake refreshed the next morning, filled with the conviction that the new day is yours to mold.

338. ✎ LET YOUR PROBLEMS WORK ON THEMSELVES

Don't begrudge yourself a few forms of escape. A distracted mind is at least better than a frustrated one. But try to see that an escape is not really an escape but a detour, like taking the long way home in order to clear out your head. Sooner or later, you're going to have to face your troubles. And the problem with distraction is not that it brings relief—which is a good thing—but that it creates divisions within the mind. Watching TV, for example, often causes one part of the mind to relax while another continues to fester with anxiety or resentment. So if you're going to check out, try to do so whole-heartedly, with the intention to find rest and strength for what needs to be done. If you can keep this in mind, you will find yourself seeking more wholesome forms of oblivion—the best of which, as the Buddha himself said, is sleep. Learn the art of a well-placed nap. Dreaming your life away won't help you, but neither will grinding against your troubles. Learn to lie down for a bit and let your problems work on themselves. That right there is a window into great wisdom.

339. ∽ The Truth Has to Taste Good

The truth has to taste good, not just be good for you. If you stop to consider that all of what we do, however skillful or misguided, is based on a desire to be happy, you begin to see that there isn't much truth in a truth that tastes horrible. A lot of us work on ourselves because we believe we've sinned and need to be forgiven. Most of us need to learn a spirituality based on innocence: to work on ourselves at the right time, for the right reasons, when we see that the work will bring us joy. A friend of mine recently told me a story about a man whose son only wanted to play video games instead of learning to read or do math. The father didn't oppose his son directly, he just waited till the day when the boy expressed a desire to become a video-game programmer. "You'll probably need to learn letters and numbers for that," his father said. And the boy did: he learned to read and do math in no time at all. So today, try to get some sense of the truths you are ready for and the ones you aren't. It's not a matter of denying any truth, but of seeing that truth always exists within time. The more you understand which conflicts you aren't ready to face, the more energy you'll have to deal with the ones you can. And that is when you'll make the leap from merely imitating a model of perfection to actually learning something for yourself.

340. ∽ This Must Be the Place

Don't forget where you are. My teacher always says, "Wherever you are is where you need to be to learn what you need to learn." We might get upset by this idea and say, "Are you suggesting that I deserve my pain, my loss, my difficulty?" But being in the right place has nothing to do with deserving anything. You do not deserve your pain, your loss, or your difficulty, yet you will meet with these things, and when you do, the gap between your life and the way your mind relates to it will be revealed. And you must remember that there is no greater blessing than to be able to see this gap and begin to close it.

So today, when you find yourself wishing you were somewhere else, remind yourself: This is the place. My senses aren't deceiving me, nor is the compass of my life in error. Be still and be patient. The thing you are waiting for will not fail to keep its appointment.

341. ∾ WE'RE ALL IN ONE BOAT

If you want to change things, you're going to have to learn how to talk with people you don't agree with—beginning with yourself. Behind all your negative emotions, there is conflict between parts of you. You feel rage when someone differs with you because part of you agrees with that person; you feel lost in your career because part of you would rather do something completely different. But you are not yourself, you are many selves, and when you start to embrace your contradictions, something wonderful happens: you begin to see that every feeling—anger, jealousy, doubt—is a messenger bringing information about what all of you needs to be happy. We sometimes speak of meditation as though it were the act of taking off dirty clothes and putting on white robes of holiness, but the reality is that meditation is simply the art of realizing, in your own mind, the truth of the old blues lyric: "We're all in one boat, brother. And if you shake one end, you gonna rock the other."

342. ∾ COUNT THE QUESTION MARKS

If you want to find more clarity in your life, make it a practice not to react to other people's taunts. Every time you react to a taunt, inwardly or outwardly, you are making a statement to yourself about what is important in your life. As the Thai ajaans would say, you are "undergoing a training." When you react defensively, you are training your mind to be on the defensive; when you react angrily, you are training your mind to be in conflict. And as the years pile up, this is how a life loses its direction. So just as you can't respond to every piece of junk mail and hope to get anything done in a day, so too you can't respond to every person's perception of you and hope to be happy. Years back, I took a job in which it was routine for clients to send long, angry emails. I couldn't not answer them, so I developed a game called Count the Question Marks, in which I replied with one sentence for every actual question the client was asking. Write me five pages of ranting containing only one real question, you get a one-sentence answer, and so forth. I soon discovered that this practice not only saved me time and grief, but actually calmed my clients down. We all want to live unhooked from one another's dramas. So today, when someone provokes you, ask yourself, "Is there really a question here?" If there isn't, free yourself from the obligation to provide an answer.

343. ∽ BORED AT THE MOVIES

Interest is a quality we bring to life, not the other way around. People find it much harder to sit quietly with themselves for an hour than to watch a bad movie for that same length of time. Is it that our minds, with their infinite complexity, are somehow less compelling than a mediocre Hollywood script? The real difference is that we watch a film expecting something to be revealed, whereas when we look at our minds, we are too preoccupied making what we find there be a certain way to actually observe what is happening. If our thoughts were movies, we would switch them off the moment any conflict came on the screen. We want sunsets and rolling credits only. In short, it is we who make ourselves dull. So today, when the work you are doing or the people you are with seem tiresome, treat your boredom as a plot-twist. Ask yourself: "What led me here?" "What am I supposed to learn?" The questions you ask are not as important as the fact that you ask questions. For in the end, no story really goes anywhere, and our stories, too, are really going nowhere, but the curious will inherit the beauty that is everywhere.

344. ∾ FEELING OLD

We feel old mostly when we forget that we are creators, not just consumers, of life. I don't think I've ever felt older than when I was twenty-three and convinced I'd tasted all of what life had to offer— and I know many people in their seventies and eighties who recall a similar weariness to their youth. We often confuse the reality of aging (and aging is a reality) with our tendency to forget that we are the ones who are shaping our lives, moment by moment, through our thoughts and intentions. Whatever the destiny of our bodies may be, the source of our deepest fertility lies is the mind and how we use it. So the real antidote to feeling old is not a cream or a diet, but practice in learning how to fabricate fruitful thoughts. You can start today by developing thoughts of generosity. Try to help some-one, and try to use that moment of giving as an opportunity to plant seeds of joy in your mind. Tell yourself you are glad you gave. Then search in your body for a sense of warmth, tenderness, or brightness that is the sprouting of the seeds you have planted. When you begin to see that you can grow mind states just as you can grow skin cells, you will never feel irrelevant or forgotten by life again. The body grows older, things keep decaying, but you are still here, alive at the center of all creation.

345. ∾ TELEPHONE BOOK

Strength is not something you simply have, but something you learn, through practice, to draw upon. When you feel weak, when you feel you can't go on, it isn't brute force that will rescue you, but rather, the ability to search for the invisible sources of support that exist all around and within you. Strength has a lot to do with memory: if you can remember what supported you in the past and remember to look for it in the present, you will never have to face your struggles alone. Athletes develop physical strength by recalling patterns of movement that have worked before, and the development of emotional strength is no different. This is why we need to practice gratitude every day—not in order to be sentimental, but to improve our memories and keep our blessings close at hand, like a book of telephone numbers that connects us to a larger network of goodness. So count your blessings today, whether or not life is going well. For tomorrow, who knows? Your dreams may not be there, but the skills you have developed will.

346. ∾ Respecting Awkwardness

Don't be in a hurry to overcome your inhibitions. Your blocks are a gift and the keepers of your life's true purpose. Respect awkwardness where you find it, and do not try to tear a wall down till you've climbed it and seen the world from its heights.

347. ∾ Life Moves Forward in Sketches

Learn to have faith in bad drafts. Artist or not, you have seen how life moves forward in sketches. The days fly furiously past, and nothing is ever perfected before it happens, only after, in hindsight and revision. But it is one of life's beautiful paradoxes that although we are given impossibly short deadlines, we are also blessed with more time than we think to rewrite. So whatever you are trying to do today, make a start at it. Get it out of you, wretched though it seems. And then, the hard part: sit with it for as long as you can bear. Walk through the city with all your incompletion; live it and breathe it in all its apparent mediocrity. Only then will you see that your world is not as solid as you supposed. Buildings keep shifting long after they are built, seeking deeper and deeper balance. Your actions keep growing long after they're done. Every life keeps on living long after it's born.

348. ∾ If You Care, You Care

It won't do any good to pretend you don't care what others think of you. If you care, you care. You have about as much control over that as you do over the weather. But what you can do is understand why you feel so endangered by other people's negative opinion of you. You may feel that way because, at some point in your life, someone or some people made you feel responsible for their happiness and blamed you for not having done enough to bring them peace of mind. And now, what stings in the criticism of others is not the content of that criticism (which might actually be useful to you,) but the sense of powerlessness you feel about not having found a way to make others happy. So if you want to find real peace, not just fake toughness, you must remind yourself: "All people are the owners of their actions. Their happiness depends on their own actions, not on my wishes for them." If you can cultivate this perception, you will find the objectivity necessary to listen to what people have to say and let in what is helpful. You will also find that you do care—not so much about your reputation, but about doing whatever needs to be done to let the light within you shine.

349. ∾ A Jigsaw Puzzle in the Hands of a Child

Try to view your past as a set of potentials. We tend to think of a life as a single, fixed story, but in reality, it is more like a jigsaw puzzle in the hands of a child: many of the pieces have been put together in the wrong order, and other important pieces have yet to be touched. In order to get some control over the big picture, you have to see that there are parts of your mind you don't yet know how to use properly. A good rule of thumb is that if something feels wrong, it probably is. For example, if you find yourself thinking painful thoughts—"I'm a failure" or "No one cares about me"—don't keep trying to make those pieces fit by telling a pretty story around them. Just say to yourself, "I guess I don't know how to use that thought yet," and set it aside. Come back to your breath. The breath is the corner piece of the puzzle, because it is the standard against which all harmony and disharmony in life can be measured. In your breath, you will see the past in all its variety and potential, for breath is simply the body's manifestation of every way you have ever hurt or healed yourself. So choose a way of breathing that feels good. If you can do that, the rest of the puzzle will piece itself together, bit by bit.

350. ∾ LOST IN WANTING TO BE FOUND

We get so lost in wanting to be found. Like bad Hollywood screen-writers, we are constantly trying to impose a narrative structure onto our lives in an attempt to find some kind of resolution: "I was a sinner but now I've found salvation," "I was lonely but now I've found love," "I was foolish but now I've found wisdom." Look at these stories. Do you see how exhausting they are to maintain, how much blood, sweat, and tears humanity has shed over them? Do you see how unsatisfactory, how empty of sustenance they really are? So today, try to remember that wisdom is not a story. Wisdom is increased sensitivity in the face of repetition—that quality of mak-ing the same mistakes over and over yet seeing more vividly each time around, until finally not making the same mistakes becomes as natural as not touching a hot stove. You are going to struggle today, but if you remember that your happiness depends on your actions, you will develop wisdom. You are going to make a mess of things today, but if you have compassion for yourself, you will develop wisdom. Try not to think about all the bridges you have burned, for all bridges fall in time. Just be vulnerable with yourself and those near to you, and you will find something better than any conclusion or closure: the opening of your heart.

351. ∾ YOUR NEWS FEED

Your mind is not so different from your tailored news feed on social media. What it shows you at any moment is not reality, but rather, the part of reality you've been preoccupied with recently. Your news feed is just the news that you feed, and your whole experience of life works this way too: what keeps re-arising in your awareness is only what you are in the habit of choosing. If you struggle with anger, for example, it is because you like your anger on some level. At some point, you have to stop running from your difficult emotions and start to understand their appeal, for until you see why part of you would choose them, you will keep on choosing them again and again. When you can have compassion for yourself for all the unskillful ways you try to make yourself happy, when you can accept yourself as a person with unresolved problems, only then can you get around to the real work of change, which is not to fight pain but to starve it. Until you find love for yourself in your heart, you will keep swinging at your misery with one hand and feeding it with the other.

352. ∾ It Never Stops

This much I know of life: it never stops. Perhaps in death it does, but till that point, which we know only by abstraction, life continues on and every moment continues to matter. Each action you take—physical, verbal, or mental—leads you either toward happiness or away from it, and there are no breaks, no vacations, no spaces free from consequence. But though the effort you must make to live well is unending, so too are the opportunities for bending your mind in the direction of joy, and you will find that the more you bend, the easier it becomes to bend even more, till like someone who has moved his hand far from the hinge of a door, you now have leverage to open your heart to every moment, whether the moment is easy or difficult. So today, when you start to feel weary, when you feel you need a break, remind yourself that there are no breaks in the unbroken flow of time, and ask yourself instead: "What can I give to this moment?" If you practice, you will see how much you do have to give: your attention, your care, your kindness. It gets easier and easier if you don't ask to be let off of work. As they say, "When you love what you do, you'll never work again."

353. ∾ In the Groove

Make the best of this day, but try not to squeeze it too much. For whatever you do, you will get exactly twenty-four hours of experience. Your fulfillment will not come from making "more" of the time, but from learning to find and live in the rhythm of the hours. Just as a musician does not try to get to the end of a song quickly but to inhabit the groove fully, see to it that you embrace whatever pace life brings you. If you feel anxious, you're probably just ahead of the beat; if you feel lazy, you're too far behind. You may disagree with the drummer's tempo, but you will not improve the music by fighting it. Just bring your attention to your breath, your first and deepest instrument, and try to breathe in a way that matches the timing of what is happening right now. If you crave peace, you can try extending your exhales. If you crave energy, you can try extending your inhales. But learn how to improvise, for the point is not just to play along with life, but to play with it. You can push against the breath or be pushed by it. There are no rules, no way life is supposed to be, only this eternal process of testing things till we discover we are free.

354. ∾ Each Moment Is a Training

Try to see each moment as a training. When it comes to our bodies, it is relatively easy for us to see the connection between what we do and how we feel. Even an inherently stressful activity such as running can be pleasurable if you understand the strength it is bringing to your physical being. But when it comes to our minds, we tend to get lost in the content of each moment: whether the train is on time, whether the food tastes good, whether the beloved has written back yet. We forget that the training of our minds depends not only on the content of experience, but also on the intentions we bring to that experience. When we bring resentment or frustration, we are training ourselves to feel that way more and more. When we bring love, that is our training too. People are always going on about "being present," but you can't be present if you focus on the content of every moment, for the present moment is often very painful. To be truly present, you have to look forward to the fruits of your training. When your heart breaks, when your body breaks, you have to see it all as an exercise—a drill for strengthening the parts of yourself that cannot be broken. For you are working toward something rare and beautiful, despite the sickness, aging, death, and separation that are coming your way. Take these shocks and use them to set yourself free.

355. ∽ VACATIONS COME TO AN END SOMETIME

Be careful of your desire for sudden transformation. We are always talking about "transformational experiences," by which we mainly mean vacations from the parts of ourselves we don't like. Vacations are good opportunities to get perspective, but they come to an end eventually, and just as energy can neither be created nor destroyed, your anger, sadness, and jealousy cannot simply be burned away in some alchemical fire. But what you can do is learn to put these impulses to work, for just as economic unemployment breeds resentment and rebellion in a nation, so too your difficult parts are only difficult because you aren't giving them anything worthwhile to do. So today, when you are disturbed by something, ask yourself, "What is this feeling for?" and understand that everything in your heart has both a reason and a skill-set. Learn to appreciate the energy and power in what you still haven't found an outlet for, and in time it will find it own gainful employment. Above all, don't ask when you'll be finished with this work. Work is dignity, so take up your burden and meet this day with grace and love.

356. ∾ FLOATING ON YOUR BACK

You don't have to make clarity happen, for clarity is a natural force, like gravity, and becomes evident as soon as you remove any opposing forces. When you were young and learned to float on your back, you discovered that the trick was not to push your body above water but to keep still enough to let your body's own lightness do the work. That is the same perspective you must have about all your difficulties. Your task is only to put yourself into position to let natural clarity rise on its own. Jung once said that every relationship has its optimal distance, and it's true: harmony between any two people is less a matter of compatibility and more a matter of knowing how far or near to be to one another, like two planets that will always stay in orbit if they are close enough to feel each other's magnetism but not too close that they repel or collide. And really, all experience is this way: not just your human relationships, but your relationship to success, to creativity, to self-improvement. So today, when you feel frustrated or confused about something, instead of asking, "How can I fix this?" ask yourself, "What is the optimal distance between me and the problem?" Sometimes it's just a matter of thinking about your troubles a little less, or showing up to what is uncomfortable a little more. Try to understand, in any case, that the world isn't weighing on your shoulders. It is spinning free on its own axis, and you are dancing on yours along with it.

357. ∾ FEAR OF MISSING OUT

Take a closer look at your exhaustion. You may work hard, but do you really work harder than your parents did or your grandparents or pioneers on the American frontier or all the peasants and slaves who have toiled throughout history? Or is it possible that your exhaustion has less to do with your body and more to do with a mind that cannot say no to any thought, like a man who has been feeding every stray cat that comes to his door and now can't get any rest because of the chorus of howling beasts outside his window? One of the most exhausting thoughts we feed is the perception that we are on the verge of missing an important opportunity. Whether it is a romantic partner or a job opening or enlightenment itself, we are always running to catch some train we are sure is about to leave the station. And so you must remind yourself that in life there are always an infinite number of trains that run according to a schedule you will never fully comprehend. As David Bowie said, "There is no journey. We are arriving and departing all at the same time." This doesn't mean there isn't work to be done, but it is a different sort of work we must learn: not the work of rushing out to catch the wind, but the work of gathering the mind in. This is the irony of meditation; the more effort we make to see that the important decisions are being made right here in the present moment, the more energy we come to have at our disposal. So today, guard against anxiety and self-pity about not having enough time or strength, and bring your mind instead to your breath. Feel the power flowing through you in every inhalation and exhalation. There are storehouses within you that you never knew existed. Tap them.

358. ∾ MINDFULNESS AND DEATH

There is no mindfulness without mindfulness of death. In our culture, mindfulness has come to mean being "really into" whatever you are doing: the fine meal you are eating or the ambitions you are pursuing. But that kind of "corporate mindfulness," as one of my teachers calls it, misses the point. You are going to die, no matter how present you are, and there are no prizes for being fully immersed in trivia. Mindfulness actually means keeping in mind what is important—your mortality, above all. When you reflect that death can come at any time, you see that your experiences are as fleeting as your possessions, and it is no better to be attached to the first than to the second. So while you must make the most of your life and try to do some of the things you have always wanted to do, you must also realize that you will never do all the things. There is something better than experience, and it is found not with your body, but within your body. If you can focus on your blessings and your heart just a little bit more, you will find the days you have left are enough. So let your mind be full of that thought today, leaving no room for worries or vain ambitions, and you will find the peace that real mindfulness brings.

359. ⌇ GROUNDHOG'S DAY

Don't waste your life waiting for other people to change. Imagine, Groundhog's Day-style, that you will relive the way things are right now with those you love, over and over, forever, with all the same joys and frustrations eternally reoccurring. If that sounds like hell, you might be in the wrong relationships. But if in this thought of eternal return you can sense a softening, if you can sense that time will eventually change other people's foibles into a language you can understand, if you can sense that one day you will have used up all the lightning of wanting think to be different and be left only with the calm after the storm—then why do you not live that way today? Don't forget, in your desire to protect and stand up for yourself, that one of the greatest expressions of self-love is not taking what others do personally. So today, if Tom annoys you, say to yourself, "Well that just Tom," and let the open-endedness of the other person's name stand for all the things you cannot control but will one day look back on and be glad could not have been otherwise.

360. ⌇ THE MIND'S TELEVISION

Belief is the mind's television: It can excite us, but not incite us. A person who believes in love is no closer to practicing it than a person watching a hospital drama is to practicing medicine.

361. ∾ TRACING PAPER

So much of learning to be happy is finding a balance between watching and doing. Most of the time we are out of balance. Sometimes we see our lives clearly but are unwilling to change them. But more often, I have found, we try to change our lives without being willing to take a step back and observe what we are actually doing. When we were young and first discovered tracing paper, we were fascinated by the simple act of copying, the joy of observing a shape and following it with our attentions and hands. Later, we learned that we were supposed to be original, and we lost touch with the pure feeling of being absorbed in observation. But it is precisely this absorption that we need to relearn in order to do great things with our lives. So today, notice where you are out of balance, and notice where you are watching or doing too little or too much. You can learn a lot about balance by focusing on your breath. Is your breath boring to watch? If so, try consciously changing it to make it more interesting. But if the problem is that your mind is too restless to watch anything, then try this: take a breath, letting it come however it wants to, and then with your second breath, try to copy the first in length, rhythm, and texture, as precisely as you can. Then let yourself breathe naturally again, and again repeat this cycle. If you stay with this dialogue for a while, you will see that it's not just a game, for what you are experiencing is yourself as both creator and receiver of your life, and right here at the tip of your nose, you are watching these roles become one. That is where the magic happens.

362. ∾ DELEGATE MORE

Learn to delegate more. A new year has begun, yet the old question remains: What will you do with your time? What will you do with the rest of your life? But before you answer with a thousand plans and resolutions, ask yourself: "What are you not going to do this year? What problems and commitments will you turn away, or at least turn over to the many powers around you that stand ready to help?" Start with your body, noticing that as you consume less, more harmony arises between the parts of your physical experience. Look at your human interactions, noticing that as you try to control others less, more cooperation arises between you and them. Growth is mainly a subtractive process, so starting today, pick a few actions you need to take and turn the rest of your anxieties and agendas over to what lies beyond you. Let your problems work on themselves for a while. For though we often try to let go, it is more important to let life be, and in letting life be, to let life help.

363. ∾ LET IRRITATION MOVE

Let your irritations move. In certain situations, around certain people, you may experience the feeling of wanting to jump out of your own skin. That is the sign of a healthy nervous system trying to bring itself into equilibrium. The problem is not that you feel irritation flowing through you, but that you fail to see that all your resentments and ideas about who is to blame for your irritation are actually a way of constricting its flow and thereby allowing it to do harm, just as an electrical current passing through a human body only does damage when it meets with resistance and is converted into heat. So today, when you find yourself getting annoyed by something or someone, try to locate this feeling of heat in your body and allow it to circulate and disperse. It's often helpful to visualize heat flowing out through your hands and feet, but other perceptions may work better for you. The important thing is to realize that the way to move stifled energy is not to push or pull it, but just to be an observer. Remind yourself, "I never asked for this irritation," and allow your awareness to separate from it as oil separates from vinegar in a bottle of salad dressing left still. You don't have to justify your annoyance or make excuses for what is coming up. It's only your human experience passing through you, and it will not hurt you or anyone else if you just let it pass away.

364. ∾ More Shall Be Revealed

Be careful about your desire for closure. We all want more clarity in our lives, relationships, and work. And yet, in trying to force things into final resolution, we often give up our freedom by acting as though the world around us must be straightened out before we change our lives from within. Remember that you are free—free to come and go as you please, free to choose your attitude, your intentions, and therefore your destiny—regardless of whether you ultimately leave or stay with your partner or job or whatever situation you are currently in. Try to understand, too, that all your agonizing over closure is actually concealing something your thinking mind cannot yet grasp. Jung once pointed out that the part of a dream most easily interpreted is also the most irrelevant, for the psyche does not express in unconscious symbols what it already consciously knows. The same is true of the dilemmas you have managed to get into: they are difficult for you precisely because more has yet to be revealed, precisely because you can't know the answers from your current perspective. So if you want to speed up the process of finding clarity, try to let go of some of your inner debating and try to love your life exactly as it is right now. Try to see the best in your job or partner or situation even as you remind yourself that you are free to go. For in learning to love what is, we take back our power and prevent ourselves from repeating the same patterns with other jobs and other partners. So today, practice tuning out the impatient voices within you and around you that say you must choose to accept, change, or leave your situation. You have one more option: to love. You can love something without accepting it forever; you can love something without being able to change it yet; you can love something without being ready to leave it. You can always love, so don't forget where your true strength resides.

365. ∾ IN OVER YOUR HEAD

Practice being in over your head. What you most want to do with your life is not anything you were born good at doing. In school, they may have taught you to go where praise and success have already paved the way: if you were good at math, somebody probably told you to go into math; if you were good at art, somebody told you to become an artist. But beyond the suburbs of your education so far, the wildness of your real life is calling. And you will learn to navigate that wildness not by jumping out of a plane or taking more classes, but by developing the mindset that every situation in every day is trying to convey some message or revelation to you. Learn to hear the thoughts in your head as though they were spoken by someone else, someone trying to alert you to something you have not yet considered. Learn to feel each breath as though your body were trying to teach you new possibilities of pleasure and ease in this physical form. Receive. For there will be time for thinking critically about what you are receiving, but critical thinking comes more easily to us than faith—not blind faith, but the faith Martin Luther King described as "taking the first step even when you don't see the whole staircase." So today, in some area of your life, try to feel your way in the dark, and listen, listen everywhere life is talking to you in languages you still do not speak. For it is in those tongues that the truth of who you are is being uttered.

Index of Themes

The Magpie Art: Gathering the Brightness of Every Day was typeset in Bembo which is a typefact that goes back to one of the most famous printers of the Renaissance, Aldus Manutius. In 1496 he used a new weight of a roman face, formed by Francesco Griffo da Bologna, to print the short piece 'De Aetna' by Pietro Bembo. This very typeface would eventually be of such importance that the development of print typefaces is unthinkable without it.

The first developmental phase was defined by the influence of the classic Roman forms, indentifiable by the slight slant of the lower case s and the high crossbar of the lower case e, which in time took on less and less of a slant. The Monotype Corporation in London used this roman face as the model for a 1929 project of Stanley Morison which resulted in a font called Bembo. Morison made a number of changes to the 15th century forms. He modified the capital G and instead of the italic which Manutius originally had in mind, he used that from a sample book written in 1524 by Giovanni Tagliente in Venice. Italic capitals came from the Roman forms.

↶